C-2913

T0325404

THIS IS YOUR **PASSBOOK**® FOR ...

NURSE ADMINISTRATOR

NATIONAL LEARNING CORPORATION®
passbooks.com

PASSBOOK® SERIES

THE *PASSBOOK® SERIES* has been created to prepare applicants and candidates for the ultimate academic battlefield – the examination room.

At some time in our lives, each and every one of us may be required to take an examination – for validation, matriculation, admission, qualification, registration, certification, or licensure.

Based on the assumption that every applicant or candidate has met the basic formal educational standards, has taken the required number of courses, and read the necessary texts, the *PASSBOOK® SERIES* furnishes the one special preparation which may assure passing with confidence, instead of failing with insecurity. Examination questions – together with answers – are furnished as the basic vehicle for study so that the mysteries of the examination and its compounding difficulties may be eliminated or diminished by a sure method.

This book is meant to help you pass your examination provided that you qualify and are serious in your objective.

The entire field is reviewed through the huge store of content information which is succinctly presented through a provocative and challenging approach – the question-and-answer method.

A climate of success is established by furnishing the correct answers at the end of each test.

You soon learn to recognize types of questions, forms of questions, and patterns of questioning. You may even begin to anticipate expected outcomes.

You perceive that many questions are repeated or adapted so that you can gain acute insights, which may enable you to score many sure points.

You learn how to confront new questions, or types of questions, and to attack them confidently and work out the correct answers.

You note objectives and emphases, and recognize pitfalls and dangers, so that you may make positive educational adjustments.

Moreover, you are kept fully informed in relation to new concepts, methods, practices, and directions in the field.

You discover that you arre actually taking the examination all the time: you are preparing for the examination by "taking" an examination, not by reading extraneous and/or supererogatory textbooks.

In short, this PASSBOOK®, used directedly, should be an important factor in helping you to pass your test.

NURSE ADMINISTRATOR

DUTIES:

As a Nurse Administrator or Nurse Administrator (Psychiatric), you would be responsible for the direction and coordination of nursing services for a large number of individuals who meet the criterion for services by the agency in which you are employed. This will involve direct and/or indirect supervision of professional and direct care staff. Your responsibilities may include ensuring implementation of facility policies and procedures related to nursing, initiating special investigations, scheduling staff, directing staff, teaching appropriate nursing techniques, and reviewing individuals' records for compliance with agency practice/protocol and developing a plan for correcting any deficiencies found.

SUBJECTS OF EXAMINATION:

The written test is designed to evaluate knowledge, skills and /or abilities in the following areas:

1. **Administrative supervision** - These questions test for knowledge of the principles and practices involved in directing the activities of a large subordinate staff, including subordinate supervisors. Questions relate to the personal interactions between an upper level supervisor and his/her subordinate supervisors in the accomplishment of objectives. These questions cover such areas as assigning work to and coordinating the activities of several units, establishing and guiding staff development programs, evaluating the performance of subordinate supervisors, and maintaining relationships with other organizational sections.

2. **Understanding and interpreting written material** - These questions test how well you comprehend written material. You will be provided with brief reading selections and will be asked questions about the selections. All the information required to answer the questions will be presented in the selections; you will not be required to have any special knowledge relating to the subject areas of the selections.

3. **Preparing written material** - These questions test for the ability to present information clearly and accurately, and to organize paragraphs logically and comprehensibly. For some questions, you will be given information in two or three sentences followed by four restatements of the information. You must then choose the best version. For other questions, you will be given paragraphs with their sentences out of order. You must then choose, from four suggestions, the best order for the sentences.

4. **Ensuring effective inter/intra agency communications** - These questions test for understanding of techniques for interacting effectively with individuals and agencies, to educate and inform them about topics of concern, to clarify agency programs or policies, to negotiate conflicts or resolve complaints, and to represent one's agency or program in a manner in keeping with good public relations practices. Questions may also cover interacting with the staff of one's own agency and/or that of other agencies in cooperative efforts of public outreach or service.

5. **Administrative techniques and practices** - These questions test for a knowledge of management techniques and practices used in directing or assisting in directing a program component or an organizational segment. Questions cover such areas as interpreting policies, making decisions based on the context of the position in the organization, coordinating programs or projects, communicating with employees or the public, planning employee training, and researching and evaluating areas of concern.

HOW TO TAKE A TEST

I. YOU MUST PASS AN EXAMINATION

A. *WHAT EVERY CANDIDATE SHOULD KNOW*

Examination applicants often ask us for help in preparing for the written test. What can I study in advance? What kinds of questions will be asked? How will the test be given? How will the papers be graded?

As an applicant for a civil service examination, you may be wondering about some of these things. Our purpose here is to suggest effective methods of advance study and to describe civil service examinations.

Your chances for success on this examination can be increased if you know how to prepare. Those "pre-examination jitters" can be reduced if you know what to expect. You can even experience an adventure in good citizenship if you know why civil service exams are given.

B. *WHY ARE CIVIL SERVICE EXAMINATIONS GIVEN?*

Civil service examinations are important to you in two ways. As a citizen, you want public jobs filled by employees who know how to do their work. As a job seeker, you want a fair chance to compete for that job on an equal footing with other candidates. The best-known means of accomplishing this two-fold goal is the competitive examination.

Exams are widely publicized throughout the nation. They may be administered for jobs in federal, state, city, municipal, town or village governments or agencies.

Any citizen may apply, with some limitations, such as the age or residence of applicants. Your experience and education may be reviewed to see whether you meet the requirements for the particular examination. When these requirements exist, they are reasonable and applied consistently to all applicants. Thus, a competitive examination may cause you some uneasiness now, but it is your privilege and safeguard.

C. *HOW ARE CIVIL SERVICE EXAMS DEVELOPED?*

Examinations are carefully written by trained technicians who are specialists in the field known as "psychological measurement," in consultation with recognized authorities in the field of work that the test will cover. These experts recommend the subject matter areas or skills to be tested; only those knowledges or skills important to your success on the job are included. The most reliable books and source materials available are used as references. Together, the experts and technicians judge the difficulty level of the questions.

Test technicians know how to phrase questions so that the problem is clearly stated. Their ethics do not permit "trick" or "catch" questions. Questions may have been tried out on sample groups, or subjected to statistical analysis, to determine their usefulness.

Written tests are often used in combination with performance tests, ratings of training and experience, and oral interviews. All of these measures combine to form the best-known means of finding the right person for the right job.

II. HOW TO PASS THE WRITTEN TEST

A. NATURE OF THE EXAMINATION

To prepare intelligently for civil service examinations, you should know how they differ from school examinations you have taken. In school you were assigned certain definite pages to read or subjects to cover. The examination questions were quite detailed and usually emphasized memory. Civil service exams, on the other hand, try to discover your present ability to perform the duties of a position, plus your potentiality to learn these duties. In other words, a civil service exam attempts to predict how successful you will be. Questions cover such a broad area that they cannot be as minute and detailed as school exam questions.

In the public service similar kinds of work, or positions, are grouped together in one "class." This process is known as *position-classification*. All the positions in a class are paid according to the salary range for that class. One class title covers all of these positions, and they are all tested by the same examination.

B. FOUR BASIC STEPS

1) Study the announcement

How, then, can you know what subjects to study? Our best answer is: "Learn as much as possible about the class of positions for which you've applied." The exam will test the knowledge, skills and abilities needed to do the work.

Your most valuable source of information about the position you want is the official exam announcement. This announcement lists the training and experience qualifications. Check these standards and apply only if you come reasonably close to meeting them.

The brief description of the position in the examination announcement offers some clues to the subjects which will be tested. Think about the job itself. Review the duties in your mind. Can you perform them, or are there some in which you are rusty? Fill in the blank spots in your preparation.

Many jurisdictions preview the written test in the exam announcement by including a section called "Knowledge and Abilities Required," "Scope of the Examination," or some similar heading. Here you will find out specifically what fields will be tested.

2) Review your own background

Once you learn in general what the position is all about, and what you need to know to do the work, ask yourself which subjects you already know fairly well and which need improvement. You may wonder whether to concentrate on improving your strong areas or on building some background in your fields of weakness. When the announcement has specified "some knowledge" or "considerable knowledge," or has used adjectives like "beginning principles of…" or "advanced … methods," you can get a clue as to the number and difficulty of questions to be asked in any given field. More questions, and hence broader coverage, would be included for those subjects which are more important in the work. Now weigh your strengths and weaknesses against the job requirements and prepare accordingly.

3) Determine the level of the position

Another way to tell how intensively you should prepare is to understand the level of the job for which you are applying. Is it the entering level? In other words, is this the position in which beginners in a field of work are hired? Or is it an intermediate or advanced level? Sometimes this is indicated by such words as "Junior" or "Senior" in the class title. Other jurisdictions use Roman numerals to designate the level – Clerk I, Clerk II, for example. The word "Supervisor" sometimes appears in the title. If the level is not indicated by the title, check the description of duties. Will you be working under very close supervision, or will you have responsibility for independent decisions in this work?

4) Choose appropriate study materials

Now that you know the subjects to be examined and the relative amount of each subject to be covered, you can choose suitable study materials. For beginning level jobs, or even advanced ones, if you have a pronounced weakness in some aspect of your training, read a modern, standard textbook in that field. Be sure it is up to date and has general coverage. Such books are normally available at your library, and the librarian will be glad to help you locate one. For entry-level positions, questions of appropriate difficulty are chosen – neither highly advanced questions, nor those too simple. Such questions require careful thought but not advanced training.

If the position for which you are applying is technical or advanced, you will read more advanced, specialized material. If you are already familiar with the basic principles of your field, elementary textbooks would waste your time. Concentrate on advanced textbooks and technical periodicals. Think through the concepts and review difficult problems in your field.

These are all general sources. You can get more ideas on your own initiative, following these leads. For example, training manuals and publications of the government agency which employs workers in your field can be useful, particularly for technical and professional positions. A letter or visit to the government department involved may result in more specific study suggestions, and certainly will provide you with a more definite idea of the exact nature of the position you are seeking.

III. KINDS OF TESTS

Tests are used for purposes other than measuring knowledge and ability to perform specified duties. For some positions, it is equally important to test ability to make adjustments to new situations or to profit from training. In others, basic mental abilities not dependent on information are essential. Questions which test these things may not appear as pertinent to the duties of the position as those which test for knowledge and information. Yet they are often highly important parts of a fair examination. For very general questions, it is almost impossible to help you direct your study efforts. What we can do is to point out some of the more common of these general abilities needed in public service positions and describe some typical questions.

1) General information

Broad, general information has been found useful for predicting job success in some kinds of work. This is tested in a variety of ways, from vocabulary lists to questions about current events. Basic background in some field of work, such as sociology or economics, may be sampled in a group of questions. Often these are principles which have become familiar to most persons through exposure rather than through formal training. It is difficult to advise you how to study for these questions; being alert to the world around you is our best suggestion.

2) Verbal ability

An example of an ability needed in many positions is verbal or language ability. Verbal ability is, in brief, the ability to use and understand words. Vocabulary and grammar tests are typical measures of this ability. Reading comprehension or paragraph interpretation questions are common in many kinds of civil service tests. You are given a paragraph of written material and asked to find its central meaning.

3) Numerical ability

Number skills can be tested by the familiar arithmetic problem, by checking paired lists of numbers to see which are alike and which are different, or by interpreting charts and graphs. In the latter test, a graph may be printed in the test booklet which you are asked to use as the basis for answering questions.

4) Observation

A popular test for law-enforcement positions is the observation test. A picture is shown to you for several minutes, then taken away. Questions about the picture test your ability to observe both details and larger elements.

5) Following directions

In many positions in the public service, the employee must be able to carry out written instructions dependably and accurately. You may be given a chart with several columns, each column listing a variety of information. The questions require you to carry out directions involving the information given in the chart.

6) Skills and aptitudes

Performance tests effectively measure some manual skills and aptitudes. When the skill is one in which you are trained, such as typing or shorthand, you can practice. These tests are often very much like those given in business school or high school courses. For many of the other skills and aptitudes, however, no short-time preparation can be made. Skills and abilities natural to you or that you have developed throughout your lifetime are being tested.

Many of the general questions just described provide all the data needed to answer the questions and ask you to use your reasoning ability to find the answers. Your best preparation for these tests, as well as for tests of facts and ideas, is to be at your physical and mental best. You, no doubt, have your own methods of getting into an exam-taking mood and keeping "in shape." The next section lists some ideas on this subject.

IV. KINDS OF QUESTIONS

Only rarely is the "essay" question, which you answer in narrative form, used in civil service tests. Civil service tests are usually of the short-answer type. Full instructions for answering these questions will be given to you at the examination. But in case this is your first experience with short-answer questions and separate answer sheets, here is what you need to know:

1) Multiple-choice Questions

Most popular of the short-answer questions is the "multiple choice" or "best answer" question. It can be used, for example, to test for factual knowledge, ability to solve problems or judgment in meeting situations found at work.

A multiple-choice question is normally one of three types—

- It can begin with an incomplete statement followed by several possible endings. You are to find the one ending which *best* completes the statement, although some of the others may not be entirely wrong.
- It can also be a complete statement in the form of a question which is answered by choosing one of the statements listed.
- It can be in the form of a problem – again you select the best answer.

Here is an example of a multiple-choice question with a discussion which should give you some clues as to the method for choosing the right answer:

When an employee has a complaint about his assignment, the action which will *best* help him overcome his difficulty is to
- A. discuss his difficulty with his coworkers
- B. take the problem to the head of the organization
- C. take the problem to the person who gave him the assignment
- D. say nothing to anyone about his complaint

In answering this question, you should study each of the choices to find which is best. Consider choice "A" – Certainly an employee may discuss his complaint with fellow employees, but no change or improvement can result, and the complaint remains unresolved. Choice "B" is a poor choice since the head of the organization probably does not know what assignment you have been given, and taking your problem to him is known as "going over the head" of the supervisor. The supervisor, or person who made the assignment, is the person who can clarify it or correct any injustice. Choice "C" is, therefore, correct. To say nothing, as in choice "D," is unwise. Supervisors have and interest in knowing the problems employees are facing, and the employee is seeking a solution to his problem.

2) True/False Questions

The "true/false" or "right/wrong" form of question is sometimes used. Here a complete statement is given. Your job is to decide whether the statement is right or wrong.

SAMPLE: A roaming cell-phone call to a nearby city costs less than a non-roaming call to a distant city.

This statement is wrong, or false, since roaming calls are more expensive.

This is not a complete list of all possible question forms, although most of the others are variations of these common types. You will always get complete directions for answering questions. Be sure you understand *how* to mark your answers – ask questions until you do.

V. RECORDING YOUR ANSWERS

Computer terminals are used more and more today for many different kinds of exams.

For an examination with very few applicants, you may be told to record your answers in the test booklet itself. Separate answer sheets are much more common. If this separate answer sheet is to be scored by machine – and this is often the case – it is highly important that you mark your answers correctly in order to get credit.

An electronic scoring machine is often used in civil service offices because of the speed with which papers can be scored. Machine-scored answer sheets must be marked with a pencil, which will be given to you. This pencil has a high graphite content which responds to the electronic scoring machine. As a matter of fact, stray dots may register as answers, so do not let your pencil rest on the answer sheet while you are pondering the correct answer. Also, if your pencil lead breaks or is otherwise defective, ask for another.

Since the answer sheet will be dropped in a slot in the scoring machine, be careful not to bend the corners or get the paper crumpled.

The answer sheet normally has five vertical columns of numbers, with 30 numbers to a column. These numbers correspond to the question numbers in your test booklet. After each number, going across the page are four or five pairs of dotted lines. These short dotted lines have small letters or numbers above them. The first two pairs may also have a "T" or "F" above the letters. This indicates that the first two pairs only are to be used if the questions are of the true-false type. If the questions are multiple choice, disregard the "T" and "F" and pay attention only to the small letters or numbers.

Answer your questions in the manner of the sample that follows:

32. The largest city in the United States is
    A. Washington, D.C.
    B. New York City
    C. Chicago
    D. Detroit
    E. San Francisco

1) Choose the answer you think is best. (New York City is the largest, so "B" is correct.)
2) Find the row of dotted lines numbered the same as the question you are answering. (Find row number 32)
3) Find the pair of dotted lines corresponding to the answer. (Find the pair of lines under the mark "B.")
4) Make a solid black mark between the dotted lines.

VI. BEFORE THE TEST

Common sense will help you find procedures to follow to get ready for an examination. Too many of us, however, overlook these sensible measures. Indeed, nervousness and fatigue have been found to be the most serious reasons why applicants fail to do their best on civil service tests. Here is a list of reminders:

- Begin your preparation early – Don't wait until the last minute to go scurrying around for books and materials or to find out what the position is all about.
- Prepare continuously – An hour a night for a week is better than an all-night cram session. This has been definitely established. What is more, a night a week for a month will return better dividends than crowding your study into a shorter period of time.
- Locate the place of the exam – You have been sent a notice telling you when and where to report for the examination. If the location is in a different town or otherwise unfamiliar to you, it would be well to inquire the best route and learn something about the building.
- Relax the night before the test – Allow your mind to rest. Do not study at all that night. Plan some mild recreation or diversion; then go to bed early and get a good night's sleep.
- Get up early enough to make a leisurely trip to the place for the test – This way unforeseen events, traffic snarls, unfamiliar buildings, etc. will not upset you.
- Dress comfortably – A written test is not a fashion show. You will be known by number and not by name, so wear something comfortable.
- Leave excess paraphernalia at home – Shopping bags and odd bundles will get in your way. You need bring only the items mentioned in the official notice you received; usually everything you need is provided. Do not bring reference books to the exam. They will only confuse those last minutes and be taken away from you when in the test room.
- Arrive somewhat ahead of time – If because of transportation schedules you must get there very early, bring a newspaper or magazine to take your mind off yourself while waiting.
- Locate the examination room – When you have found the proper room, you will be directed to the seat or part of the room where you will sit. Sometimes you are given a sheet of instructions to read while you are waiting. Do not fill out any forms until you are told to do so; just read them and be prepared.
- Relax and prepare to listen to the instructions
- If you have any physical problem that may keep you from doing your best, be sure to tell the test administrator. If you are sick or in poor health, you really cannot do your best on the exam. You can come back and take the test some other time.

VII. AT THE TEST

The day of the test is here and you have the test booklet in your hand. The temptation to get going is very strong. Caution! There is more to success than knowing the right answers. You must know how to identify your papers and understand variations in the type of short-answer question used in this particular examination. Follow these suggestions for maximum results from your efforts:

1) Cooperate with the monitor

The test administrator has a duty to create a situation in which you can be as much at ease as possible. He will give instructions, tell you when to begin, check to see that you are marking your answer sheet correctly, and so on. He is not there to guard you, although he will see that your competitors do not take unfair advantage. He wants to help you do your best.

2) Listen to all instructions

Don't jump the gun! Wait until you understand all directions. In most civil service tests you get more time than you need to answer the questions. So don't be in a hurry. Read each word of instructions until you clearly understand the meaning. Study the examples, listen to all announcements and follow directions. Ask questions if you do not understand what to do.

3) Identify your papers

Civil service exams are usually identified by number only. You will be assigned a number; you must not put your name on your test papers. Be sure to copy your number correctly. Since more than one exam may be given, copy your exact examination title.

4) Plan your time

Unless you are told that a test is a "speed" or "rate of work" test, speed itself is usually not important. Time enough to answer all the questions will be provided, but this does not mean that you have all day. An overall time limit has been set. Divide the total time (in minutes) by the number of questions to determine the approximate time you have for each question.

5) Do not linger over difficult questions

If you come across a difficult question, mark it with a paper clip (useful to have along) and come back to it when you have been through the booklet. One caution if you do this – be sure to skip a number on your answer sheet as well. Check often to be sure that you have not lost your place and that you are marking in the row numbered the same as the question you are answering.

6) Read the questions

Be sure you know what the question asks! Many capable people are unsuccessful because they failed to *read* the questions correctly.

7) Answer all questions

Unless you have been instructed that a penalty will be deducted for incorrect answers, it is better to guess than to omit a question.

8) Speed tests

It is often better NOT to guess on speed tests. It has been found that on timed tests people are tempted to spend the last few seconds before time is called in marking answers at random – without even reading them – in the hope of picking up a few extra points. To discourage this practice, the instructions may warn you that your score will be "corrected" for guessing. That is, a penalty will be applied. The incorrect answers will be deducted from the correct ones, or some other penalty formula will be used.

9) Review your answers

If you finish before time is called, go back to the questions you guessed or omitted to give them further thought. Review other answers if you have time.

10) Return your test materials

If you are ready to leave before others have finished or time is called, take ALL your materials to the monitor and leave quietly. Never take any test material with you. The monitor can discover whose papers are not complete, and taking a test booklet may be grounds for disqualification.

VIII. EXAMINATION TECHNIQUES

1) Read the general instructions carefully. These are usually printed on the first page of the exam booklet. As a rule, these instructions refer to the timing of the examination; the fact that you should not start work until the signal and must stop work at a signal, etc. If there are any *special* instructions, such as a choice of questions to be answered, make sure that you note this instruction carefully.

2) When you are ready to start work on the examination, that is as soon as the signal has been given, read the instructions to each question booklet, underline any key words or phrases, such as *least*, *best*, *outline*, *describe* and the like. In this way you will tend to answer as requested rather than discover on reviewing your paper that you *listed without describing*, that you selected the *worst* choice rather than the *best* choice, etc.

3) If the examination is of the objective or multiple-choice type – that is, each question will also give a series of possible answers: A, B, C or D, and you are called upon to select the best answer and write the letter next to that answer on your answer paper – it is advisable to start answering each question in turn. There may be anywhere from 50 to 100 such questions in the three or four hours allotted and you can see how much time would be taken if you read through all the questions before beginning to answer any. Furthermore, if you come across a question or group of questions which you know would be difficult to answer, it would undoubtedly affect your handling of all the other questions.

4) If the examination is of the essay type and contains but a few questions, it is a moot point as to whether you should read all the questions before starting to answer any one. Of course, if you are given a choice – say five out of seven and the like – then it is essential to read all the questions so you can eliminate the two that are most difficult. If, however, you are asked to answer all the questions, there may be danger in trying to answer the easiest one first because you may find that you will spend too much time on it. The best technique is to answer the first question, then proceed to the second, etc.

5) Time your answers. Before the exam begins, write down the time it started, then add the time allowed for the examination and write down the time it must be completed, then divide the time available somewhat as follows:

- If 3-1/2 hours are allowed, that would be 210 minutes. If you have 80 objective-type questions, that would be an average of 2-1/2 minutes per question. Allow yourself no more than 2 minutes per question, or a total of 160 minutes, which will permit about 50 minutes to review.
- If for the time allotment of 210 minutes there are 7 essay questions to answer, that would average about 30 minutes a question. Give yourself only 25 minutes per question so that you have about 35 minutes to review.

6) The most important instruction is to *read each question* and make sure you know what is wanted. The second most important instruction is to *time yourself properly* so that you answer every question. The third most important instruction is to *answer every question*. Guess if you have to but include something for each question. Remember that you will receive no credit for a blank and will probably receive some credit if you write something in answer to an essay question. If you guess a letter – say "B" for a multiple-choice question – you may have guessed right. If you leave a blank as an answer to a multiple-choice question, the examiners may respect your feelings but it will not add a point to your score. Some exams may penalize you for wrong answers, so in such cases *only*, you may not want to guess unless you have some basis for your answer.

7) Suggestions
   a. Objective-type questions
      1. Examine the question booklet for proper sequence of pages and questions
      2. Read all instructions carefully
      3. Skip any question which seems too difficult; return to it after all other questions have been answered
      4. Apportion your time properly; do not spend too much time on any single question or group of questions
      5. Note and underline key words – *all, most, fewest, least, best, worst, same, opposite,* etc.
      6. Pay particular attention to negatives
      7. Note unusual option, e.g., unduly long, short, complex, different or similar in content to the body of the question
      8. Observe the use of "hedging" words – *probably, may, most likely,* etc.
      9. Make sure that your answer is put next to the same number as the question
      10. Do not second-guess unless you have good reason to believe the second answer is definitely more correct
      11. Cross out original answer if you decide another answer is more accurate; do not erase until you are ready to hand your paper in
      12. Answer all questions; guess unless instructed otherwise
      13. Leave time for review

   b. Essay questions
      1. Read each question carefully
      2. Determine exactly what is wanted. Underline key words or phrases.
      3. Decide on outline or paragraph answer

4. Include many different points and elements unless asked to develop any one or two points or elements
5. Show impartiality by giving pros and cons unless directed to select one side only
6. Make and write down any assumptions you find necessary to answer the questions
7. Watch your English, grammar, punctuation and choice of words
8. Time your answers; don't crowd material

8) Answering the essay question

Most essay questions can be answered by framing the specific response around several key words or ideas. Here are a few such key words or ideas:

M's: manpower, materials, methods, money, management
P's: purpose, program, policy, plan, procedure, practice, problems, pitfalls, personnel, public relations

  a. Six basic steps in handling problems:
    1. Preliminary plan and background development
    2. Collect information, data and facts
    3. Analyze and interpret information, data and facts
    4. Analyze and develop solutions as well as make recommendations
    5. Prepare report and sell recommendations
    6. Install recommendations and follow up effectiveness

  b. Pitfalls to avoid
    1. *Taking things for granted* – A statement of the situation does not necessarily imply that each of the elements is necessarily true; for example, a complaint may be invalid and biased so that all that can be taken for granted is that a complaint has been registered
    2. *Considering only one side of a situation* – Wherever possible, indicate several alternatives and then point out the reasons you selected the best one
    3. *Failing to indicate follow up* – Whenever your answer indicates action on your part, make certain that you will take proper follow-up action to see how successful your recommendations, procedures or actions turn out to be
    4. *Taking too long in answering any single question* – Remember to time your answers properly

IX. AFTER THE TEST

Scoring procedures differ in detail among civil service jurisdictions although the general principles are the same. Whether the papers are hand-scored or graded by machine we have described, they are nearly always graded by number. That is, the person who marks the paper knows only the number – never the name – of the applicant. Not until all the papers have been graded will they be matched with names. If other tests, such as training and experience or oral interview ratings have been given, scores will be combined. Different parts of the examination usually have different weights. For example, the written test might count 60 percent of the final grade, and a rating of training and experience 40 percent. In many jurisdictions, veterans will have a certain number of points added to their grades.

After the final grade has been determined, the names are placed in grade order and an eligible list is established. There are various methods for resolving ties between those who get the same final grade – probably the most common is to place first the name of the person whose application was received first. Job offers are made from the eligible list in the order the names appear on it. You will be notified of your grade and your rank as soon as all these computations have been made. This will be done as rapidly as possible.

People who are found to meet the requirements in the announcement are called "eligibles." Their names are put on a list of eligible candidates. An eligible's chances of getting a job depend on how high he stands on this list and how fast agencies are filling jobs from the list.

When a job is to be filled from a list of eligibles, the agency asks for the names of people on the list of eligibles for that job. When the civil service commission receives this request, it sends to the agency the names of the three people highest on this list. Or, if the job to be filled has specialized requirements, the office sends the agency the names of the top three persons who meet these requirements from the general list.

The appointing officer makes a choice from among the three people whose names were sent to him. If the selected person accepts the appointment, the names of the others are put back on the list to be considered for future openings.

That is the rule in hiring from all kinds of eligible lists, whether they are for typist, carpenter, chemist, or something else. For every vacancy, the appointing officer has his choice of any one of the top three eligibles on the list. This explains why the person whose name is on top of the list sometimes does not get an appointment when some of the persons lower on the list do. If the appointing officer chooses the second or third eligible, the No. 1 eligible does not get a job at once, but stays on the list until he is appointed or the list is terminated.

X. HOW TO PASS THE INTERVIEW TEST

The examination for which you applied requires an oral interview test. You have already taken the written test and you are now being called for the interview test – the final part of the formal examination.

You may think that it is not possible to prepare for an interview test and that there are no procedures to follow during an interview. Our purpose is to point out some things you can do in advance that will help you and some good rules to follow and pitfalls to avoid while you are being interviewed.

What is an interview supposed to test?

The written examination is designed to test the technical knowledge and competence of the candidate; the oral is designed to evaluate intangible qualities, not readily measured otherwise, and to establish a list showing the relative fitness of each candidate – as measured against his competitors – for the position sought. Scoring is not on the basis of "right" and "wrong," but on a sliding scale of values ranging from "not passable" to "outstanding." As a matter of fact, it is possible to achieve a relatively low score without a single "incorrect" answer because of evident weakness in the qualities being measured.

Occasionally, an examination may consist entirely of an oral test – either an individual or a group oral. In such cases, information is sought concerning the technical knowledges and abilities of the candidate, since there has been no written examination for this purpose. More commonly, however, an oral test is used to supplement a written examination.

Who conducts interviews?

The composition of oral boards varies among different jurisdictions. In nearly all, a representative of the personnel department serves as chairman. One of the members of the board may be a representative of the department in which the candidate would work. In some cases, "outside experts" are used, and, frequently, a businessman or some other representative of the general public is asked to serve. Labor and management or other special groups may be represented. The aim is to secure the services of experts in the appropriate field.

However the board is composed, it is a good idea (and not at all improper or unethical) to ascertain in advance of the interview who the members are and what groups they represent. When you are introduced to them, you will have some idea of their backgrounds and interests, and at least you will not stutter and stammer over their names.

What should be done before the interview?

While knowledge about the board members is useful and takes some of the surprise element out of the interview, there is other preparation which is more substantive. It *is* possible to prepare for an oral interview – in several ways:

1) Keep a copy of your application and review it carefully before the interview

This may be the only document before the oral board, and the starting point of the interview. Know what education and experience you have listed there, and the sequence and dates of all of it. Sometimes the board will ask you to review the highlights of your experience for them; you should not have to hem and haw doing it.

2) Study the class specification and the examination announcement

Usually, the oral board has one or both of these to guide them. The qualities, characteristics or knowledges required by the position sought are stated in these documents. They offer valuable clues as to the nature of the oral interview. For example, if the job involves supervisory responsibilities, the announcement will usually indicate that knowledge of modern supervisory methods and the qualifications of the candidate as a supervisor will be tested. If so, you can expect such questions, frequently in the form of a hypothetical situation which you are expected to solve. NEVER go into an oral without knowledge of the duties and responsibilities of the job you seek.

3) Think through each qualification required

Try to visualize the kind of questions you would ask if you were a board member. How well could you answer them? Try especially to appraise your own knowledge and background in each area, *measured against the job sought*, and identify any areas in which you are weak. Be critical and realistic – do not flatter yourself.

4) Do some general reading in areas in which you feel you may be weak

For example, if the job involves supervision and your past experience has NOT, some general reading in supervisory methods and practices, particularly in the field of human relations, might be useful. Do NOT study agency procedures or detailed manuals. The oral board will be testing your understanding and capacity, not your memory.

5) Get a good night's sleep and watch your general health and mental attitude

You will want a clear head at the interview. Take care of a cold or any other minor ailment, and of course, no hangovers.

What should be done on the day of the interview?

Now comes the day of the interview itself. Give yourself plenty of time to get there. Plan to arrive somewhat ahead of the scheduled time, particularly if your appointment is in the fore part of the day. If a previous candidate fails to appear, the board might be ready for you a bit early. By early afternoon an oral board is almost invariably behind schedule if there are many candidates, and you may have to wait. Take along a book or magazine to read, or your application to review, but leave any extraneous material in the waiting room when you go in for your interview. In any event, relax and compose yourself.

The matter of dress is important. The board is forming impressions about you – from your experience, your manners, your attitude, and your appearance. Give your personal appearance careful attention. Dress your best, but not your flashiest. Choose conservative, appropriate clothing, and be sure it is immaculate. This is a business interview, and your appearance should indicate that you regard it as such. Besides, being well groomed and properly dressed will help boost your confidence.

Sooner or later, someone will call your name and escort you into the interview room. *This is it.* From here on you are on your own. It is too late for any more preparation. But remember, you asked for this opportunity to prove your fitness, and you are here because your request was granted.

What happens when you go in?

The usual sequence of events will be as follows: The clerk (who is often the board stenographer) will introduce you to the chairman of the oral board, who will introduce you to the other members of the board. Acknowledge the introductions before you sit down. Do not be surprised if you find a microphone facing you or a stenotypist sitting by. Oral interviews are usually recorded in the event of an appeal or other review.

Usually the chairman of the board will open the interview by reviewing the highlights of your education and work experience from your application – primarily for the benefit of the other members of the board, as well as to get the material into the record. Do not interrupt or comment unless there is an error or significant misinterpretation; if that is the case, do not hesitate. But do not quibble about insignificant matters. Also, he will usually ask you some question about your education, experience or your present job – partly to get you to start talking and to establish the interviewing "rapport." He may start the actual questioning, or turn it over to one of the other members. Frequently, each member undertakes the questioning on a particular area, one in which he is perhaps most competent, so you can expect each member to participate in the examination. Because time is limited, you may also expect some rather abrupt switches in the direction the questioning takes, so do not be upset by it. Normally, a board member will not pursue a single line of questioning unless he discovers a particular strength or weakness.

After each member has participated, the chairman will usually ask whether any member has any further questions, then will ask you if you have anything you wish to add. Unless you are expecting this question, it may floor you. Worse, it may start you off on an extended, extemporaneous speech. The board is not usually seeking more information. The question is principally to offer you a last opportunity to present further qualifications or to indicate that you have nothing to add. So, if you feel that a significant qualification or characteristic has been overlooked, it is proper to point it out in a sentence or so. Do not compliment the board on the thoroughness of their examination – they have been sketchy, and you know it. If you wish, merely say, "No thank you, I have nothing further to add." This is a point where you can "talk yourself out" of a good impression or fail to present an important bit of information. Remember, *you close the interview yourself.*

The chairman will then say, "That is all, Mr. _____, thank you." Do not be startled; the interview is over, and quicker than you think. Thank him, gather your belongings and take your leave. Save your sigh of relief for the other side of the door.

How to put your best foot forward

Throughout this entire process, you may feel that the board individually and collectively is trying to pierce your defenses, seek out your hidden weaknesses and embarrass and confuse you. Actually, this is not true. They are obliged to make an appraisal of your qualifications for the job you are seeking, and they want to see you in your best light. Remember, they must interview all candidates and a non-cooperative candidate may become a failure in spite of their best efforts to bring out his qualifications. Here are 15 suggestions that will help you:

1) Be natural – Keep your attitude confident, not cocky

If you are not confident that you can do the job, do not expect the board to be. Do not apologize for your weaknesses, try to bring out your strong points. The board is interested in a positive, not negative, presentation. Cockiness will antagonize any board member and make him wonder if you are covering up a weakness by a false show of strength.

2) Get comfortable, but don't lounge or sprawl

Sit erectly but not stiffly. A careless posture may lead the board to conclude that you are careless in other things, or at least that you are not impressed by the importance of the occasion. Either conclusion is natural, even if incorrect. Do not fuss with your clothing, a pencil or an ashtray. Your hands may occasionally be useful to emphasize a point; do not let them become a point of distraction.

3) Do not wisecrack or make small talk

This is a serious situation, and your attitude should show that you consider it as such. Further, the time of the board is limited – they do not want to waste it, and neither should you.

4) Do not exaggerate your experience or abilities

In the first place, from information in the application or other interviews and sources, the board may know more about you than you think. Secondly, you probably will not get away with it. An experienced board is rather adept at spotting such a situation, so do not take the chance.

5) If you know a board member, do not make a point of it, yet do not hide it

Certainly you are not fooling him, and probably not the other members of the board. Do not try to take advantage of your acquaintanceship – it will probably do you little good.

6) Do not dominate the interview

Let the board do that. They will give you the clues – do not assume that you have to do all the talking. Realize that the board has a number of questions to ask you, and do not try to take up all the interview time by showing off your extensive knowledge of the answer to the first one.

7) Be attentive

You only have 20 minutes or so, and you should keep your attention at its sharpest throughout. When a member is addressing a problem or question to you, give him your undivided attention. Address your reply principally to him, but do not exclude the other board members.

8) Do not interrupt

A board member may be stating a problem for you to analyze. He will ask you a question when the time comes. Let him state the problem, and wait for the question.

9) Make sure you understand the question

Do not try to answer until you are sure what the question is. If it is not clear, restate it in your own words or ask the board member to clarify it for you. However, do not haggle about minor elements.

10) Reply promptly but not hastily

A common entry on oral board rating sheets is "candidate responded readily," or "candidate hesitated in replies." Respond as promptly and quickly as you can, but do not jump to a hasty, ill-considered answer.

11) Do not be peremptory in your answers

A brief answer is proper – but do not fire your answer back. That is a losing game from your point of view. The board member can probably ask questions much faster than you can answer them.

12) Do not try to create the answer you think the board member wants

He is interested in what kind of mind you have and how it works – not in playing games. Furthermore, he can usually spot this practice and will actually grade you down on it.

13) Do not switch sides in your reply merely to agree with a board member

Frequently, a member will take a contrary position merely to draw you out and to see if you are willing and able to defend your point of view. Do not start a debate, yet do not surrender a good position. If a position is worth taking, it is worth defending.

14) Do not be afraid to admit an error in judgment if you are shown to be wrong

The board knows that you are forced to reply without any opportunity for careful consideration. Your answer may be demonstrably wrong. If so, admit it and get on with the interview.

15) Do not dwell at length on your present job

The opening question may relate to your present assignment. Answer the question but do not go into an extended discussion. You are being examined for a *new* job, not your present one. As a matter of fact, try to phrase ALL your answers in terms of the job for which you are being examined.

Basis of Rating

Probably you will forget most of these "do's" and "don'ts" when you walk into the oral interview room. Even remembering them all will not ensure you a passing grade. Perhaps you did not have the qualifications in the first place. But remembering them will help you to put your best foot forward, without treading on the toes of the board members.

Rumor and popular opinion to the contrary notwithstanding, an oral board wants you to make the best appearance possible. They know you are under pressure – but they also want to see how you respond to it as a guide to what your reaction would be under the pressures of the job you seek. They will be influenced by the degree of poise you display, the personal traits you show and the manner in which you respond.

ABOUT THIS BOOK

This book contains tests divided into Examination Sections. Go through each test, answering every question in the margin. At the end of each test look at the answer key and check your answers. On the ones you got wrong, look at the right answer choice and learn. Do not fill in the answers first. Do not memorize the questions and answers, but understand the answer and principles involved. On your test, the questions will likely be different from the samples. Questions are changed and new ones added. If you understand these past questions you should have success with any changes that arise. Tests may consist of several types of questions. We have additional books on each subject should more study be advisable or necessary for you. Finally, the more you study, the better prepared you will be. This book is intended to be the last thing you study before you walk into the examination room. Prior study of relevant texts is also recommended. NLC publishes some of these in our Fundamental Series. Knowledge and good sense are important factors in passing your exam. Good luck also helps. So now study this Passbook, absorb the material contained within and take that knowledge into the examination. Then do your best to pass that exam.

———

EXAMINATION SECTION

EXAMINATION SECTION
TEST 1

DIRECTIONS: Each question or incomplete statement is followed by several suggested answers or completions. Select the one that BEST answers the question or completes the statement. *PRINT THE LETTER OF THE CORRECT ANSWER IN THE SPACE AT THE RIGHT.*

1. Each nursing supervisor should work with his or her head nurses to determine the staff requirement for each unit. They should consider all of the following EXCEPT the _____ of the unit.

   A. past experiences
   B. anticipated needs
   C. length or size
   D. percentage of occupancy

   1.____

2. The estimation of staff for each unit does NOT need to include

   A. provisions for vacations
   B. sick leave
   C. overtime pay
   D. on-call pay

   2.____

3. Problems of cost increase of primary nursing could be overcome by the practice of

   A. assessing present staffing to bring it to an acceptable standard of patient care hours
   B. upgrading positions as vacancies occur
   C. utilizing all levels of staff more effectively
   D. all of the above

   3.____

4. The_____ forecasting method employs the upside/downside concept and seeks to project realistic figures based on the impact of demands for services.

   A. mechanical
   B. analytical
   C. historic
   D. qualitative

   4.____

5. Critical factors to be considered in forecasting are future events or conditions that will affect

   A. situation
   B. people
   C. time
   D. all of the above

   5.____

6. If you notice or experience price variance in supplies, you should determine the

   A. reasons causing price increase and whether the price increase is permanent or temporary
   B. availability of substitute supplies
   C. feasibility of reducing price through the bidding process or other purchase techniques
   D. all of the above

   6.____

7. Manager education regarding the control of resources should involve all of the following EXCEPT

   A. salary education
   B. financial education
   C. responsibility
   D. accountability

   7.____

8. To educate a manager regarding accountability, one should NOT   8.____

    A. clarify accountability
    B. provide positive support
    C. provide consistent feedback
    D. fail to enforce accountability

9. The fundamental elements of the nursing delivery system include   9.____

    A. clinical decision making
    B. work allocation
    C. communication
    D. all of the above

Questions 10-16.

DIRECTIONS: Answer Questions 10 through 16 using the following choices:

    A. Functional system
    B. Case system
    C. Primary care system
    D. Team system

10. The OLDEST method of delivering nursing care is the _____.   10.____

11. The MOST frequently adopted method of delivering nursing care is the _____.   11.____

12. The MOST recently developed nursing care delivery method is the _____.   12.____

13. One nurse is involved in nursing observation and care of a single patient. This system of delivering nursing care is termed the _____.   13.____

14. The nursing care delivery system that focuses on the number of tasks that must be provided to the overall patient population is called the _____.   14.____

15. When different members of the nursing staff do tasks for a given patient, they employ the_____.   15.____

16. The MOST comprehensive care, in terms of patient's need, is BEST provided by the _____.   16.____

17. The objectives of team nursing include providing   17.____

    A. adequate staff for good care
    B. good experiences for staff members
    C. good personnel policies to maintain morale
    D. all of the above

18. The case system of delivering nursing care is PRIMARILY used for assignments in the   18.____

    A. outpatient clinic   B. inpatient clinic
    C. intensive care unit   D. home

19. In the primary care delivery system, the _____ make(s) the final decision about nursing care of assigned patients.

    A. team leader
    B. primary nurse
    C. head nurse
    D. different nurses

19.____

20. A team member, as a part of team nursing, should do all of the following EXCEPT

    A. when reporting for duty, obtain a written assignment
    B. receive verbal or taped reports on the team's patients
    C. plan care for the next shift
    D. take orders from nursing care plans and doctor's order sheet

20.____

21. Of the following, the one which does NOT have to be considered when making team nursing assignments is

    A. ethnic background of patients
    B. qualitative work load
    C. quantitative work load
    D. geography of unit

21.____

22. The primary nurse is a registered professional nurse, responsible and accountable for all of the following EXCEPT

    A. the nursing process for a specified number of patients
    B. delivery of care 24 hours a day from admission to discharge
    C. all patients in the given unit
    D. participation in a communication triad between patient and physician

22.____

23. Which of the following is NOT among the key points regarding primary care nursing?

    A. Continuity of patient care
    B. Accountability to peers, the patient, and the physician
    C. Role model for the patient
    D. Patient inclusion in planning care

23.____

24. The cooperative care system of nursing

    A. allows the patient to maintain a passive role, receiving assistance and guidance from health care professionals
    B. has patient education as its primary therapeutic tool
    C. eliminates the need for professional nurses, eventually
    D. suggests that a home-like environment is not therapeutic to a patient's convalescence

24.____

25. In the cooperative care model, the staff nurses MUST possess

    A. a registered nurse license
    B. a wide knowledge of various medical and surgical specialties
    C. excellent communication skills
    D. all of the above

25.____

KEY (CORRECT ANSWERS)

1.	C		11.	A
2.	C		12.	C
3.	D		13.	B
4.	B		14.	A
5.	D		15.	A
6.	D		16.	C
7.	B		17.	D
8.	D		18.	C
9.	D		19.	B
10.	B		20.	C

21.	A
22.	C
23.	C
24.	B
25.	D

TEST 2

DIRECTIONS: Each question or incomplete statement is followed by several suggested answers or completions. Select the one that BEST answers the question or completes the statement. *PRINT THE LETTER OF THE CORRECT ANSWER IN THE SPACE AT THE RIGHT.*

1. All of the following are components of nursing case management EXCEPT

   A. accountability for the clinical and financial outcomes of patients' entire episodes of care
   B. the use of a caregiver as a case manager
   C. formal RN-MD group practices
   D. none of the above

   1.____

2. Paramount to the nursing care management model is the use of

   A. formal RN-MD group practices
   B. the caregiver as a case manager
   C. increased patient and family participation in and control of health care
   D. accountability

   2.____

3. Increased patient and family participation in and control of health care is achieved by

   A. pre- and post-hospitalization phone calls
   B. giving patients copies of their critical paths
   C. negotiating meaningful outcomes and discharge plans
   D. all of the above

   3.____

4. The case manager is NOT expected to

   A. establish a mechanism for notification when a new patient enters the caseload
   B. complete a follow-up evaluation
   C. begin assessment, set goals, and make plans independent of the physician
   D. introduce self to the patient or family and explain the role of case manager and group practice

   4.____

5. Potential benefits of differentiated nursing practice include all of the following EXCEPT

   A. effective deployment of nursing staff into emerging new roles
   B. decreased demand for physicians
   C. increased clinical management skills
   D. shared governance that facilitates staff nurse involvement in the clinical decision-making process

   5.____

6. Cooperative care is a method of delivering nursing care to patients who

   A. require intensive care
   B. need 24 hour a day nursing observation
   C. do not require intensive or 24 hour a day observation
   D. come to the hospital for day surgery

   6.____

7. Guidelines for designing nursing forms include:　　　　　　　　　　　　　　7.____

    A. Determine the purpose of the form
    B. Identify benefits that will be derived from introduction of the form into the record
    C. Design the form as simply as possible
    D. All of the above

8. _____ does NOT affect nursing staffing.　　　　　　　　　　　　　　8.____

    A. Characteristics of staff
    B. Ethnicity and racial background of staff and patients
    C. Trends in nursing care delivery
    D. The presence of unionization

9. The suggested nurse/patient ratio for ALL shifts, 24 hours a day, 7 days a week, in coop-　　9.____
erative care nursing is 1:

    A. 8　　　　　　B. 4　　　　　　C. 2　　　　　　D. 1

10. In the cooperative care nursing delivery system, a nurse coordinator has all of the follow-　　10.____
ing support persons EXCEPT a(n)

    A. associate director of nursing
    B. assistant nurse coordinator
    C. physician
    D. unit manager

11. The direct link between the coordinator in the cooperative care system and the executive　　11.____
director of nursing services and other hospital administrators is the

    A. assistant director of nursing
    B. associate director of nursing
    C. unit manager
    D. medical director

12. All of the following are components of the nursing care process EXCEPT　　　　12.____

    A. assessment and planning　　　　B. implementation
    C. education　　　　　　　　　　　D. evaluation

13. Assessment components of the nursing care process include all of the following　　13.____
EXCEPT

    A. history　　　　　　　　　　　　B. treatment
    C. physical examination　　　　　　D. nursing diagnosis

14. The functions of the planning component of the nursing care process include　　14.____

    A. assigning priority to the problem diagnosed
    B. differentiating problems
    C. designating specific actions
    D. all of the above

15. The planning phase begins with 15.____

    A. nursing diagnosis
    B. assessment
    C. development of nursing care plans
    D. evaluation

16. The planning phase of the nursing care process terminates with 16.____

    A. nursing diagnosis
    B. development of nursing care plans
    C. implementation
    D. evaluation

17. The development of a nursing care plan is the blueprint for 17.____

    A. action
    B. providing direction for implementing the plan
    C. providing the framework for evaluation
    D. all of the above

18. Once a nursing care plan has been developed, _____ begins. 18.____

    A. evaluation   B. assessment
    C. implementation   D. accountability

19. The implementation component of the nursing care process draws heavily on _____ nursing skills. 19.____

    A. intellectual   B. interpersonal
    C. technical   D. all of the above

20. Significant skills that enhance the success of the implementation component of the nursing care process include all of the following EXCEPT 20.____

    A. decision making   B. social attitude
    C. observation   D. communication

21. The INCORRECT statement regarding the evaluation component of nursing care is: It 21.____

    A. is expressed in terms of expected behavioral manifestations within the client
    B. indicates the degree to which the nursing diagnosis and nursing actions have been correct
    C. does not help to diagnose any new problems
    D. helps the nurse and the client to determine which problems have been resolved and which need to be reprocessed

22. A nursing diagnosis which focuses on a patient is a 22.____

    A. physiological condition combined with a problem
    B. pathophysiological response to a problem
    C. physical or behavioral response to a problem
    D. verbal response to a disease process

23. ADVANTAGES of nursing diagnoses include   23._____

    A. assisting in organizing, defining, and developing nursing knowledge
    B. facilitating the evaluation of the nursing process
    C. focusing nursing care on the patient's responses to problems
    D. all of the above

24. For effective utilization of a nursing care plan, it is important to   24._____

    A. clearly define nursing care objectives
    B. have supportive policies
    C. have administrative support
    D. all of the above

25. The successful development and carrying out of a nursing care plan for a patient   25._____
depends upon knowledge of all of the following EXCEPT the patient's

    A. financial status   B. background
    C. personality   D. illness

KEY (CORRECT ANSWERS)

1.	D		11.	B
2.	B		12.	C
3.	D		13.	B
4.	C		14.	D
5.	B		15.	A
6.	C		16.	B
7.	D		17.	D
8.	B		18.	C
9.	A		19.	D
10.	C		20.	B

21.	C
22.	C
23.	D
24.	D
25.	A

EXAMINATION SECTION
TEST 1

1. Discharge planning is dependent upon the   1._____

    A. degree of illness
    B. expected outcome of care
    C. duration and/or length of care
    D. all of the above

2. Advantages of a preadmission planning program include all of the following EXCEPT   2._____

    A. familiarizing patients and their families with the available community resources
    B. helping decrease the length of the stay
    C. estimating the cost of treatment
    D. preventing unnecessary admissions

3. A discharge planning nurse should do all of the following EXCEPT   3._____

    A. screen and study preadmission records
    B. interview, on admission, only Medicaid patients
    C. assess patients' home situations relative to discharge planning
    D. assess patients' needs, encourage self-expression, self-evaluation, and self-determination

4. A nurse should counsel and involve the patient and/or family with regard to   4._____

    A. discharge planning
    B. acceptance of illness, disability, and needed treatment
    C. coping with illness complicated by social and emotional problems
    D. all of the above

5. A nurse should recommend and assist in the placement of a patient in a nursing home but would NOT be expected to   5._____

    A. take care of any problems while in the nursing home after discharge
    B. arrange transportation if necessary
    C. inform and interpret Medicare, Medicaid, welfare, and community resources
    D. use community resources to supplement and reinforce discharge planning activities of the hospital

6. While arranging discharge planning, a nurse should make referrals to all of the following EXCEPT   6._____

    A. community health agencies
    B. the public health department
    C. the Social Security department
    D. psychiatric social workers

7. A discharge planning nurse functions as a liaison between the 　　　　　　　7.____

    A. hospital and community
    B. social service department and other community agencies
    C. doctors and patients and families
    D. all of the above

8. A discharge planning nurse functions as a resource for all of the following EXCEPT 　　8.____

    A. patient education, incorporating available facilities such as a public health nurse
    B. available community facilities
    C. financial availability for patient's family
    D. discharge planning for physician and hospital staff

9. Of the following patients, only _____ will probably NOT need discharge planning. 　　9.____

    A. those who are dependent for activities of daily life
    B. teenagers post-pneumonia
    C. patients with special teaching needs
    D. terminal or preterminal patients

10. Patients with _____ usually need discharge planning on an acute medical unit. 　　10.____

    A. arthritis 　　　　　　　　　　B. bronchiolitis
    C. cancer 　　　　　　　　　　　D. congestive heart failure

11. Steps for determining a unit's need for nursing information include 　　11.____

    A. understanding department objectives
    B. identifying information required to measure performance
    C. determining the information requirements for each decision
    D. all of the above

12. Computer applications for nursing administration include use in 　　12.____

    A. scheduling 　　　　　　　　　B. communication
    C. education 　　　　　　　　　　D. all of the above

13. Nurses hope that computers will eventually provide all of the following EXCEPT 　　13.____

    A. intelligent scheduling systems for staff and patient operative procedure
    B. treatment
    C. automated statistical reporting capabilities
    D. automated policy and with manual procedure

14. The key feature of successful future medical information systems will be the broadly 　　14.____
based integration of all of the following components EXCEPT

    A. therapeutic 　　　　　　　　　B. clinical
    C. administrative 　　　　　　　　D. financial data

15. The one of the following characteristics that is NOT essential for an effective automated 　　15.____
patient classification system is that it be

    A. objective 　　　　　　　　　　B. quick to compute for the user
    C. inflexible 　　　　　　　　　　D. simple

16. A computerized patient classification system can be used to perform all of the following tasks EXCEPT

    A. determining changes in patient mix in a given unit
    B. automating the procedures for patient care
    C. automating the procedure for determining nursing care hours
    D. determining staff mix ratio based on intensity

16.____

17. The MAJOR categories of clinical applications of a computerized information system include

    A. charting functions related to the patient's medical record
    B. selected medical and nursing requirements for the evaluation of the quality and appropriateness of patient care
    C. clinical information screens
    D. all of the above

17.____

18. All of the following are true regarding managerial reporting EXCEPT:

    A. It should focus on activities rather than achievements
    B. Quantifiable data should be used whenever possible
    C. Reports should be concise
    D. A consistent report format should be selected and used

18.____

19. Patients are generally NOT assigned to nurses

    A. geographically   B. racially
    C. individually   D. promotionally

19.____

20. All of the following are disadvantages of the geographic method of assigning patients EXCEPT

    A. no guarantee of fair caseload
    B. well organized
    C. nurse loses patient when transferred to another district
    D. unclear who is accountable when off duty for long stretches

20.____

21. Which of the following is NOT among the advantages of the geographic method of assigning patients?

    A. Stable; easy to keep track of patients
    B. Easier to have consistent secondary coverage
    C. Easier for health team to learn who has what patient
    D. No guarantee of fair caseload

21.____

22. All of the following are advantages of the individual method of assigning patients EXCEPT

    A. fair caseload
    B. much time spent in making original and daily assignments
    C. variety of cases
    D. can be maintained when readmitted

22.____

23. The individual method of assigning patients is controlled by the   23.____

    A. head nurse   B. team leader
    C. primary nurse   D. nursing supervisor

24. Advantages of the promotional method of assigning patients include all of the following   24.____
EXCEPT

    A. screening process; only for best professionals
    B. viewed as higher status
    C. large caseload
    D. increased role clarity

25. Disadvantages of the promotional method of assigning patients include   25.____
      I. much delegation of direct patient care
      II. cost of positions
      III. stimulates staff to show competence
      IV. holds back advancement if more nurses are ready to be promoted than positions available
The CORRECT answer is:

    A. I, III   B. I, II, III
    C. I, II, IV   D. II, IV

KEY (CORRECT ANSWERS)

1.	D		11.	D
2.	C		12.	D
3.	B		13.	B
4.	D		14.	A
5.	A		15.	C
6.	C		16.	B
7.	D		17.	D
8.	C		18.	A
9.	B		19.	B
10.	B		20.	B

21.	D
22.	B
23.	A
24.	C
25.	C

TEST 2

DIRECTIONS: Each question or incomplete statement is followed by several suggested answers or completions. Select the one that BEST answers the question or completes the statement. *PRINT THE LETTER OF THE CORRECT ANSWER IN THE SPACE AT THE RIGHT.*

1. All of the following are true regarding decentralization in staffing EXCEPT that it

    A. maximizes utilization of float pool
    B. maximizes unit staffing
    C. gives head nurse accountability for the entire staffing budget
    D. assigns selection of all unit staff members to head nurse

1._____

2. It is NOT true that centralization in staffing

    A. manages staffing of nursing departments as a whole
    B. maximizes utilization of float pool
    C. gives the head nurse responsibility for 24 hour staffing and scheduling
    D. centralizes updated record of skills required

2._____

3. Centralization in staffing

    A. puts decision-making in the central office
    B. eliminates a centralized float pool
    C. provides that the head nurse keeps updated record of current staff skills
    D. commits staff to making method successful

3._____

4. Decentralization in staffing

    A. gives the head nurse responsibility for 24 hour patient care
    B. assigns core unit staff selection to the head nurse
    C. promotes relationships among sister units
    D. depends more on central office management for success

4._____

5. A nursing service administrator is advised to employ _____ for establishing a staffing program.

    A. organization of a committee of the nursing staff for purposes of becoming informed about staffing
    B. appointment of an individual to assume responsibility of the program
    C. collection of data about patients
    D. all of the above

5._____

6. The coordinator of the staffing study committee carries out all of the following activities EXCEPT

    A. educating the members only
    B. instructing and supervising the study team
    C. preparing study materials and data collection forms
    D. preparing the study report

6._____

7. The activities of head nurse selected for a study committee include all of the following EXCEPT

7._____

A. classifying patients according to indicator and guidelines for nursing care requirements
B. preparing the study report
C. assisting the study coordinator in checking observer reports
D. orienting patients to the study

8. The policies and procedures for which the staffing study committee would be responsible include a

    8._____

A. written statement of the purpose, philosophy, and objectives of the nursing program of care
B. written statement of the purpose, philosophy, and objectives of staffing
C. set of performance standards for the nursing staff
D. all of the above

9. The difficulty of staffing lies in the range of variable factors that affect selecting a staffing system, such as

    9._____

A. organizational system
B. patient unit arrangement
C. employment policies
D. all of the above

10. The CENTRAL document in the staff utilization control system for staffing is the

    10._____

A. nursing staff table
B. weekly nursing utilization report
C. monthly nursing utilization report
D. staffing requirement report

11. Components of patient classification systems include all of the following EXCEPT

    11._____

A. utilization by nursing personnel
B. rigidity
C. ability to be tracked to provide staffing and acuity patterns
D. compatibility with nursing philosophy and productivity goals

12. The _____ method is NOT a type of patient classification methods.

    12._____

A. checklist of nursing tasks
B. patient needs
C. hospital needs
D. descriptive

13. Which of the following patient classification methods is probably the OLDEST? The _____ method.

    13._____

A. patient needs
B. descriptive
C. checklist of nursing tasks
D. none of the above

14. In the descriptive patient classification system, the patients who require MINIMAL care   14.____
are those who

    A. are recovering from the immediate effects of a serious illness
    B. are convalescing and no longer require intensive, moderate, and maximum care
    C. need close attention throughout the shift
    D. are acutely ill

15. In the descriptive patient classification system, the patients classified as requiring MOD-   15.____
ERATE care are those who

    A. are convalescing
    B. are recovering from the immediate effects of a serious illness
    C. are in the intensive eare unit
    D. need close attention 24 hours a day

16. In the descriptive patient classification system, the patients requiring INTENSIVE care   16.____
are those who

    A. are convalescing
    B. are recovering from a disease
    C. need close attention 24 hours a day
    D. have a high level of nurse dependency

17. Patients who require only a MINIMAL amount of nursing care, according to the patient   17.____
needs classification system, include all of the following EXCEPT those

    A. who are mildly ill
    B. whose extreme symptoms have subsided or not yet appeared
    C. who require little treatment and/or observation and/or instruction
    D. without intravenous therapy or many medications

18. According to the patient needs classification system, a patient who requires an AVER-   18.____
AGE amount of nursing care is one who

    A. required periodic treatments and/or observations and/or instructions
    B. is mildly ill
    C. requires little treatment and/or observations and/or instructions
    D. is without intravenous therapy

19. According to the patient needs classification system, patients who require ABOVE   19.____
AVERAGE nursing care would include all of the following EXCEPT the patient who

    A. is moderately ill
    B. requires treatment as frequently as every two to four hours
    C. is mildly ill
    D. is on complete bed rest

20. Patients who require MAXIMUM care, according to the patient needs classification sys-   20.____
tem, would include all of the following EXCEPT the patient

    A. who is acutely ill
    B. whose activity must be rigidly controlled
    C. who is on complete bed rest
    D. with significant changes in doctor's orders more than six times a day

Questions 21-25.

DIRECTIONS: In Questions 21 through 25, match the numbered definition with the lettered term, listed in the column below, that it BEST describes.

A. Planning variance
B. Attrition
C. Unit supervisor
D. Layoff
E. Efficiency variance

21. Difference between the required staffing and the actual staffing   21._____

22. Measures the effectiveness of the utilization forecast procedure in reporting the system   22._____
of controlling the effectiveness of the staffing system

23. Over a reasonable time period, only essential vacancies are filled   23._____

24. Termination of job after all other attempts at trimming personnel have been exhausted   24._____

25. Coordinates and supervises administrative management functions for one unit   25._____

KEY (CORRECT ANSWERS)

1.	A	11.	B
2.	C	12.	C
3.	A	13.	B
4.	C	14.	B
5.	D	15.	B
6.	A	16.	D
7.	B	17.	B
8.	D	18.	A
9.	D	19.	C
10.	B	20.	C

21.	E
22.	A
23.	B
24.	D
25.	C

EXAMINATION SECTION
TEST 1

DIRECTIONS: Each question or incomplete statement is followed by several suggested answers or completions. Select the one that BEST answers the question or completes the statement. *PRINT THE LETTER OF THE CORRECT ANSWER IN THE SPACE AT THE RIGHT.*

1. Nonroutine, nonpredictable occurrences which cause difficulties in assessing staff requirements do NOT include

    A. unexpected physician's visits and orders
    B. patients going *sour*
    C. observation of previously unidentified patient needs
    D. none of the above

1.____

2. In the manpower planning process, one should NOT

    A. analyze the present supply situation by making an inventory of the work force
    B. analyze the short-term demand situation only
    C. evaluate and update the manpower forecast
    D. reevaluate and update the manpower forecast periodically

2.____

3. Techniques for measuring a nurse's activities do NOT include a(n)

    A. time study and task frequency study
    B. work sampling of nurse activity
    C. continuous observation of nurses performing activities
    D. estimate based on other nurse's activities

3.____

4. The objectives of scheduling and allocation procedures are to assign working days and days off to individual members of the nursing staff so that

    A. adequate patient care is ensured while overstaffing is avoided
    B. a desirable distribution of days off is achieved
    C. individual members of the nursing staff are treated fairly
    D. all of the above

4.____

5. All of the following are factors that should play a part in scheduling decisions EXCEPT

    A. the different levels of nursing staff
    B. nursing coverage should be provided for at least five working days
    C. weekend days off are highly prized by nursing staff
    D. despite a salary differential, evening and night shifts are more difficult to staff

5.____

6. A scheduling system can be assessed by observing how well it functions in terms of all of the following EXCEPT

    A. coverage   B. quality   C. quantity   D. stability

6.____

7. The ability of a scheduling system to handle changes is its

    A. coverage   B. flexibility
    C. quality   D. cost

7.____

8. The measure of a schedule's desirability as judged by the nurse who will have to work it   8.____
   is called its

   A. quality   B. coverage   C. quantity   D. flexibility

9. The number of nurses assigned to be on duty is in relation to the minimum number of   9.____
   nurses required.
   This is called

   A. coverage   B. flexibility   C. fairness   D. stability

10. The guidelines for good scheduling do NOT include that   10.____

    A. the schedule should represent a balance between the needs of the employee and
       the employer
    B. the schedule should distribute only *bad* days off among all employees
    C. all employees should adhere to the established rotation
    D. advance posting of time schedules allows employees to plan their personal lives

11. All of the following are constraints that cause difficulties in making schedules EXCEPT   11.____

    A. the number of weekends off - 1 in four, 1 in three, or every other weekend
    B. no maximum length of consecutive days worked
    C. whether days off should be together or split
    D. payroll and overtime considerations

12. All of the following are true about scheduling EXCEPT   12.____

    A. there is no one schedule that will work for all hospitals and all departments
    B. select several different schedules that complement each other and develop the
       best cyclical schedule for your department
    C. do not experiment with a combination of different schedules
    D. giving more or less of one variable affects the ability to give more or less of the oth-
       ers

13. The line functions for which the nurses in management positions should be responsible   13.____
    do NOT include

    A. establishing and controlling the personnel budget
    B. developing procedures for adjustment of staff on a daily basis
    C. primary care responsibility for a patient
    D. hiring, promoting, disciplining, and discharging employees

14. The staff functions for which the central scheduling office is responsible do NOT include   14.____

    A. gathering facts and preparing reports for line personnel to facilitate budgeting
    B. hiring and discharging staff
    C. implementing procedures for position control
    D. maintaining records needed by line managers for evaluation

15. One of the drawbacks of decentralized scheduling is that   15.____

    A. nurses have more input into staffing patterns
    B. the responsibility for staffing is entrusted to the unit supervisor
    C. the unit supervisor is not an expert in staffing methods
    D. the unit supervisor is aware of the clinical needs and personal needs of staff
       nurses

16. To implement a self-scheduling system, the head nurse sets up a series of meetings to   16._____

    A. identify problems with the existing scheduling system
    B. present self-scheduling as an alternative system
    C. establish a few practice sessions with self-scheduling
    D. all of the above

17. The following are true regarding employees working under a total flextime arrangement   17._____
EXCEPT

    A. they may come and go as they please
    B. their work should be dependent on the work of others
    C. they need only to put in whatever total hours required of them for the work week
    D. they are required to accomplish the work expected of them

18. A flextime arrangement that allows workers the option of establishing their own starting   18._____
and quitting times is called

    A. total flextime   B. team flextime
    C. limited flextime   D. job sharing

19. Two or more people working part-time and mutually arranging their schedules so as to fill   19._____
one single position is called

    A. mutual flextime   B. total flextime
    C. job sharing   D. team flextime

20. One MAJOR advantage of the traditional approach to scheduling is   20._____

    A. stability   B. flexibility   C. coverage   D. quality

Questions 21-25.

DIRECTIONS: In Questions 21 through 25, match the nursing management positions in Column I with their respective job description.

COLUMN I
    A. Nursing service director
    B. Assistant nursing service director
    C. Supervisor nurse
    D. Head nurse
    E. Clinical nurse specialist

21. Direct and supervise nursing staff in provision of nursing care and ensure the availability   21._____
of support services which facilitate this care.

22. Assist in organizing and administering the department of nursing.   22._____

23. Supervise and coordinate activities of nursing personnel engaged in specific nursing services.   23._____

24. Organize and administer the department of nursing.   24._____

25. Does not have authority over the other personnel, often responsible to nursing service   25._____
director.

KEY (CORRECT ANSWERS)

1.	D		11.	B
2.	B		12.	C
3.	D		13.	C
4.	D		14.	B
5.	B		15.	C
6.	C		16.	D
7.	B		17.	B
8.	A		18.	C
9.	A		19.	C
10.	B		20.	B

21.	D
22.	B
23.	C
24.	A
25.	E

———————

TEST 2

1. The advantages of computer-aided traditional scheduling include

    A.   the flexibility of the traditional approach
    B.   reducing operating costs considerably
    C.   producing high-quality schedules consistently
    D.   all of the above

1.____

2. Cyclical scheduling, once established, has all of the following advantages EXCEPT

    A.   it meets everyday staffing requirements
    B.   the amount of highly skilled professional time spent on scheduling functions is reduced
    C.   the *good* and *bad* days off are spread equitably among all employees
    D.   schedules are known in advance by each employee

2.____

3. Disadvantages of the traditional approach to scheduling do NOT include

    A.   rigidity   B.   uneven coverage
    C.   poor quality   D.   instability

3.____

4. Disadvantages of a cyclical approach to scheduling include

    A.   low quality   B.   uneven coverage
    C.   inflexibility   D.   instability

4.____

5. The MAJOR disadvantage of a cyclical approach to scheduling is

    A.   high cost   B.   rigidity
    C.   uneven coverage   D.   time consumption

5.____

6. Which of the following is an ADVANTAGE of an 8-hour shift schedule?

    A.   It does not allow staff to have every other weekend off.
    B.   It does not permit the employee to have several consecutive days off.
    C.   The body does not have to adjust to an extended work day.
    D.   It results in unsafe traveling times

6.____

7. Advantages of a 10-hour shift schedule do NOT include that

    A.   it allows for several consecutive days off
    B.   it requires more employees than 8-hour and 12-hour shift schedules
    C.   employees can have more weekends off
    D.   individuals on different shifts have an opportunity to work together

7.____

8. The principal benefits of the seven on - seven off shift include   8._____

    A. increased utilization of space and equipment
    B. improved service to patients
    C. greatly reduced absenteeism
    D. all of the above

9. To overcome understaffing, nursing departments should establish *sister* units - cross-training groups that are comparable and related.   9._____
Examples of cross-training groups include

    A. labor, delivery, and postpartum care nurses, newborn nursery, pediatrics
    B. neonatal I.C.U. and pediatric I.C.U.
    C. intensive care unit, coronary care unit, and emergency care unit
    D. all of the above

10. Advantages of part-time work may include all of the following EXCEPT   10._____

    A. broadening an individual's horizons beyond home or school
    B. an increase in income
    C. a decrease in continuity of patient care
    D. ego satisfaction

11. Per diem nurses are hired by the hospital to work as needed.   11._____
Advantages of per diem nursing include

    A. scheduling flexibility
    B. more money per hour than career or part-time nurses
    C. the opportunity to fill in when staff are needed to work
    D. all of the above

12. The first and most obvious advantage of using temporary help agencies is the   12._____

    A. quality of care
    B. cost
    C. stable supply
    D. reduced need for orientation

13. Basic areas that should be addressed while developing a staff reduction plan include   13._____

    A. indicators for decision regarding staff reduction
    B. options and alternative plans
    C. criteria for determining employees to be reduced
    D. all of the above

14. If time permits, staffing can be adjusted on a long-term basis through attrition.   14._____
Such action can be difficult if

    A. the rate of attrition, department wide, is low
    B. the rate of attrition in a given unit is low
    C. the time to achieve reduction is short
    D. all of the above

15. The LAST step in downsizing the staff should be   15.____

    A.   temporary early retirement
    B.   elimination of management positions
    C.   terminations
    D.   attrition

16. If time allows, the FIRST step in downsizing staff should be   16.____

    A.   termination
    B.   attrition
    C.   conversion of a number of full-time to part-time positions
    D.   temporary early retirement

17. All of the following are true about the laying off of people as a measure of downsizing the   17.____
    staff EXCEPT

    A.   it should be the last resort after all other attempts have been made
    B.   employees should not be given a thorough explanation of the circumstances
    C.   employees should be advised that as circumstances change, they will again be
        considered for employment
    D.   employees should be fully informed about their unemployment status

18. The MAJOR characteristics of an effective, high quality, cost effective nursing depart-   18.____
    ment include

    A.   delivery related features
    B.   evaluation related features
    C.   policy related features
    D.   all of the above

19. Evaluation related features of the cost and quality effective nursing department include   19.____
    all of the following EXCEPT

    A.   a consumer feedback mechanism
    B.   supervisor and peer evaluations
    C.   a working relationship between nurses
    D.   a nursing question and answer program

20. A patient with many medications, IV piggybacks, and who requires hourly vital sign mon-   20.____
    itoring and/or hourly output monitoring, according to the patient's needs classification
    system, is the one who requires _____ nursing care.

    A.   maximum   B.   above average
    C.   average   D.   minimal

Questions 21-25.

DIRECTIONS: In Questions 21 through 25, match the nursing positions in Column I with their respective job descriptions.

<u>COLUMN I</u>
A.   Staff nurse
B.   Patient care technician
C.   Nursing aid
D.   Licensed practical nurse
E.   Nursing assistant

21.   Performs various patient care activities and related nonprofessional services necessary   21._____
in caring for the personal needs and comfort of patients.

22.   Renders professional nursing care to patients on an assigned unit.   22._____

23.   Performs a wide variety of patient care activities and accomodative services for assigned   23._____
hospital patients as directed by head nurse.

24.   Works under direct supervision of a registered nurse.   24._____

25.   Performs same job duties as nursing aid.   25._____

_____

KEY (CORRECT ANSWERS)

1.	D		11.	D
2.	A		12.	B
3.	A		13.	D
4.	C		14.	D
5.	B		15.	C
6.	C		16.	B
7.	B		17.	B
8.	D		18.	D
9.	D		19.	C
10.	C		20.	A

21.	C
22.	A
23.	D
24.	B
25.	E

_____

EXAMINATION SECTION
TEST 1

DIRECTIONS: Each question or incomplete statement is followed by several suggested answers or completions. Select the one that BEST answers the question or completes the statement. *PRINT THE LETTER OF THE CORRECT ANSWER IN THE SPACE AT THE RIGHT.*

1. When problems in communication have been identified, the nurse and client can set goals and begin planning ways to promote effective communication. Specific nursing interventions do NOT include

    A. developing listening skills
    B. becoming aware of how people respond
    C. establishing a formal tone
    D. all of the above

1.____

2. Resistance to change is not merely lack of acceptance but behavior intended to maintain the status quo and to prevent change.
According to New and Couillard, people resist change for all of the following reasons EXCEPT

    A. threatened self-interest
    B. inaccurate perceptions
    C. objective disagreement with the change
    D. high level of adaptability

2.____

3. Stevens described different stages of resistance to change, including all of the following EXCEPT

    A. undifferentiated resistance arises from one source
    B. the sides for and against the change line up and develop their stands
    C. the people for the change are in power
    D. the people against the change begin the stages of acceptance

3.____

4. Reinhard offers all of the following guidelines for dealing with resistance EXCEPT:

    A. Communicate with the people who oppose the change and identify the cause of their opposition
    B. Clarify information and give accurate feedback
    C. Decrease psychological security and reduce threat to it
    D. Maintain a climate of trust, support, and confidence

4.____

5. Motivation relates to whether the client wants to learn and is usually greatest when the client is ready, the learning need is recognized, and the content is meaningful to the client.
Nurses can positively influence a client's motivation by

    A. relating the learning to something the client values and helping the client see the relevance of the learning
    B. helping the client to make the learning situation pleasant
    C. encouraging self-direction
    D. all of the above

5.____

6. Written and verbal communication between health team members is vital to the quality of   6.____
health care. Accurate complete communication serves several purposes, which include
all of the following EXCEPT

    A. helps coordinate care given by several people
    B. prevents the client from having to repeat information to each health team member
    C. presumes accuracy in the provision of care and increases the possibility of error
    D. helps health personnel make the best use of their time by avoiding overlapping of
       activities

7. In a problem oriented medical record, data about the client is recorded and arranged   7.____
according to the problems the client has rather than according to the source of information. Its basic components include all of the following EXCEPT

    A. defined database
    B. initial list of orders or care plans
    C. progress notes
    D. physician's order sheet

8. Specific ways in which an automated client care plan can facilitate the role of the nurse   8.____
includes

    A. entry of nursing assessments is highly complex
    B. system facilitates complete and legible medication orders
    C. use of nursing diagnosis is exacerbated, multiple formats are utilized
    D. all of the above

9. Nursing care rounds are procedures in which a group of nurses visit all or selected   9.____
patients at their bedside in order to obtain all of the following EXCEPT

    A. information that will help plan nursing care
    B. information about ambulatory care services
    C. an opportunity for patients to discuss their care
    D. an evaluation of the nursing care the patient has received

10. Not all data that a nurse obtains about a client can be recorded.   10.____
The following guide may assist nurses in selecting essential and complete information
to record about clients, including any

    A. behavior changes
    B. retention of physical function
    C. statements made to the patient
    D. all of the above

11. Nursing diagnosis is advocated for all of the following reasons EXCEPT to   11.____

    A. aid in identifying and describing the domain and scope of nursing practice
    B. help the doctor in planning for rehabilitation care
    C. prescribe the contents of nursing curricula
    D. lead to more comprehensive and individualized patient care

12. To facilitate the implementation of nursing care plans, appropriate procedures and poli-   12.____
cies need to be established within the department of nursing itself.
These should be concerned with matters including questions concerning

    A. who has the responsibility for initiating a nursing care plan
    B. how new staff members are to be oriented
    C. what forms are to be used and where they shall be kept
    D. all of the above

13. Another step in identifying specific program needs is to determine what the cost will be.   13.____
Factors to consider in determining the cost of an educational program include all of the
following EXCEPT

    A. audiovisuals needed, e.g., movies, filmstrips, charts
    B. orthopaedic workshop budget
    C. duplicating costs, e.g., patient information booklets, pamphlets
    D. possible involvement of other departments

14. Nursing department staff will need information sessions so that they can actively support   14.____
those staff members who are teaching.
Included in the in-service sessions for the teaching staff should be all of the following
EXCEPT

    A. modes of psychoanalysis
    B. purpose of the patient education program
    C. objectives and contents
    D. methods of conveying the content

15. Discharge planning is dependent upon   15.____

    A. unexpected outcomes of care
    B. freedom from complications
    C. the availability of resources
    D. all of the above

16. The leadership style adopted by the manager depends a great deal upon all of the follow-   16.____
ing factors EXCEPT the

    A. importance of results
    B. characteristics of workers
    C. personal characteristics of the manager
    D. resources available

17. Strategies that could help a newly appointed chief nursing officer include all of the follow-   17.____
ing EXCEPT

    A. deciding on objectives and sharing them symbolically
    B. developing positive coalitions quickly
    C. minimizing the use of personal charisma to reach your constituents and not relying
       on it
    D. knowing the institutional legacy

18. The purpose of control is to see that actual performance corresponds to that which is called for in various plans. All effective managers exercise control by

18.____

    A. knowing or establishing the standards that relate to a particular course of action
    B. demanding consistent performance above the established standards
    C. punishing all deviations from the standards
    D. all of the above

19. The mutually supportive relationship between the CEO and the CNO can be enhanced by following which of the following practical suggestions?

19.____

    A. Detect potential problems and delegate their resolution to subordinate staff
    B. Disregard your visibility
    C. Foster and maintain a positive and active relationship with the medical staff
    D. All of the above

20. Among the influence strategies that effectively channel the elements of the leader's power into productive results are all of the following EXCEPT

20.____

    A. obtaining and sharing accurate information
    B. discouraging subordinates from identifying with the leader
    C. using rewards and punishments effectively
    D. understanding how to manipulate cues affecting a decision

21. The different phases of the planning process are interdependent and continuous; they frequently overlap in time and often are not discrete.
Viewed in phases, the planning process consists of

21.____

    A. seeking common purposes and objectives
    B. identifying issues and concerns
    C. determining an organizational structure for planning
    D. all of the above

22. To design and create a planning mechanism adapted to your department's conditions and needs, you must do all of the following EXCEPT

22.____

    A. pinpoint data and information needs and availability
    B. avoid setting a tentative timetable
    C. estimate budgetary requirements
    D. identify leaders and select participants for functional tasks

23. The use of data from existing sources presents few problems and precludes elaborate, time-consuming data collection.
Use of this data involves

23.____

    A. identifying their sources
    B. presuming their relevance, timeliness, and accuracy
    C. analyzing the meaning and implications of the data in terms of personal liability
    D. all of the above

24. It is difficult to anticipate the kinds of special studies that may have to be undertaken for a specific planning activity.
Special studies have been conducted in all of the following areas EXCEPT

    A. patient need for services
    B. salaries and fringe benefits
    C. ambulatory care services
    D. processes of recruitment for nursing

24.____

25. Administering a questionnaire, perhaps the most widely used method for original data collection, is the simplest type of data-collecting method.
Questionnaires are used to elicit data on all of the following EXCEPT

    A. objective facts   B. subjective facts
    C. behavioral variables   D. specified events

25.____

KEY (CORRECT ANSWERS)

1.	C	11.	B
2.	D	12.	D
3.	A	13.	B
4.	C	14.	A
5.	D	15.	C
6.	C	16.	D
7.	D	17.	C
8.	B	18.	A
9.	B	19.	C
10.	A	20.	B

21.	D
22.	B
23.	A
24.	C
25.	B

TEST 2

DIRECTIONS: Each question or incomplete statement is followed by several suggested answers or completions. Select the one that BEST answers the question or completes the statement. *PRINT THE LETTER OF THE CORRECT ANSWER IN THE SPACE AT THE RIGHT.*

1. When recommendations have been formulated and priorities have been determined, they are then incorporated into a definitive plan for meeting nursing needs.
   In developing the plan, attention is given to

   A. specifying goals, objectives, and policies for carrying out recommendations and suggested programs
   B. indicating the individuals responsible for carrying out each recommendation
   C. specifying a time span for achieving specific objectives or steps in the plan
   D. all of the above

   1.____

2. A plan is good or generally acceptable if it contains all of the following characteristics EXCEPT

   A. is in line with a clearly stated objective
   B. does not allow for alternate courses of action
   C. represents an integrated whole and not an isolated entity
   D. indicates the procedural method for putting the plan into action

   2.____

3. Resisters should become *targets* of the administrator's strategy for making an effective change.
   The administrator should take which of the following steps?

   A. Focus targets' attention on the present, not the future
   B. Assign roles, tasks, and responsibilities to others so target feels pressure to change
   C. Identify anchors who targets can trust and who will remain constant and provide stability
   D. All of the above

   3.____

4. Health system engineers are employed by hospitals and other health care institutions to study facility design and utilization, information flow, and personnel utilization.
   Activities summarizing the services provided by system engineers include

   A. analysis, design, and improvement of work systems, centers, and methods
   B. simplification of paperwork and the design of forms
   C. improvement of organizational structure, authority-responsibility relationships, and patterns of communication
   D. all of the above

   4.____

5. A system is defined as a network of interrelated operations joined together to perform an activity.
   An effective system should produce all of the following important results EXCEPT

   A. the right information furnished to the right people at the right time, and at the right cost
   B. a decrease in uncertainty and improvement of decision quality
   C. a decreased capacity to process the present and future volume of work
   D. an ability to perform profitable work that was previously impossible

   5.____

6. Styles writes that nursing organizations must perform functions for the preservation and development of the profession, including   6.____

    A. professional definition and regulation through the setting and enforcing of standards of education and practice for the generalist and specialist
    B. development of the knowledge base for practice in only broadest components
    C. defining the legal ramifications of nursing standards and limiting liability at all costs
    D. all of the above

7. The ANA Commission on Nursing Research identifies all of the following as priorities for nursing research EXCEPT   7.____

    A. promoting health and preventing illness
    B. increasing the negative impact of health problems on coping abilities, productivity, and satisfaction
    C. developing strategies that provide effective nursing care to high-risk and vulnerable groups
    D. developing cost-efficient delivery systems of nursing care

8. Nursing involves an interrelationship between many people concerned with a client's responses to potential or actual health problems.
Nursing practice involves four areas related to health, including all of the following EXCEPT   8.____

    A. health promotion   B. ambulatory care
    C. health restoration   D. care of the dying

9. Although all graduate schools have somewhat different requirements, common requirements for admission to graduate programs in nursing do NOT include that the applicant must   9.____

    A. be a registered nurse
    B. give evidence of scholastic ability
    C. score in the top 20% on a qualifying examination
    D. all of the above

10. The term *continuing education* refers to formalized experiences designed to enlarge the knowledge or skills of practitioners.
Continuing education is usually designed to   10.____

    A. keep nurses abreast of new techniques and knowledge
    B. help nurses through enhancing their research skills
    C. provide nurses with information essential to avoid legal liability
    D. all of the above

11. Socialization can be defined as the process by which people learn to become members of society.
All of the following are characteristics of socialization EXCEPT it   11.____

    A. is a reciprocal learning process brought about by interaction with other people
    B. does not establish boundaries of behavior
    C. develops a social self or awareness of others and their expectations
    D. is basic to group continuity and stability

12. Professional or occupational socialization is a very important part of adult socialization.   12.____
    The professional education concept of the nurse is one who

    A. defines clients in terms of their economic potential
    B. views the relationship between the nurse and client as a therapeutic and analytic process
    C. accepts legal responsibility and accountability for client health and welfare
    D. all of the above

13. It is within the nursing education program that professional values are developed, clari-   13.____
    fied, and internalized. Watson outlined values critical for the profession of nursing, which include all of the following EXCEPT

    A. a strong commitment to the service that nursing provides for the public
    B. belief in the dignity and worth of each person
    C. autonomy
    D. professional socialization

14. Several models have been developed to explain the initial process of socialization into   14.____
    professional roles.
    Ida Harper Simpson outlined three distinct phases of professional socialization, which include all of the following EXCEPT

    A. psyching out and role stimulation
    B. person concentrates on becoming proficient in specific work tasks
    C. person becomes attached to significant others in the work or reference group
    D. person internalizes the values of the professional group and adopts the prescribed behaviors

15. Hinshaw provided a three-phase general model of socialization that was an adaptation of   15.____
    Simpson's model.
    This model includes all of the following EXCEPT

    A. transition of anticipatory role expectations to role expectations of a societal group
    B. attachment to significant other/label incongruencies
    C. initial innocence
    D. internalization of role values

16. An advocate pleads the cause of another or argues or pleads for a cause or proposal.   16.____
    Underlying client advocacy is the belief that individuals have the right to

    A. select values they deem necessary to sustain their lives
    B. exercise judgment of the best course of action to achieve the chosen value
    C. dispose of values in a way they choose without coercion by others
    D. all of the above

17. A change agent is a person or group who initiates changes or who assists others in mak-   17.____
    ing modifications in themselves or in the system.
    Lancaster and Lancaster describe the function of a change agent in assisting a group as

    A.   determining if a problem exists
    B.   deciding on the appropriate course of action
    C.   helping to develop an evaluation format
    D.   all of the above

18.   Nursing leadership is defined as the process of interpersonal influences through which a   18.____
client is assisted in the establishment and achievement of goals towards improved well-
being.
The purposes of leadership vary according to the level of application and include all of
the following EXCEPT

    A.   improving the health status of individuals or families
    B.   increasing the effectiveness and level of satisfaction among professional col-
leagues who provide care
    C.   improving the attitudes of citizens and legislators toward the nursing profession
and their expectations of it
    D.   providing increasing home care services

19.   Participative leadership is an approach to group leadership in which functions are distrib-   19.____
uted. Participative leaders are guided by the principles that

    A.   leadership is concentrated in one primary member of the group
    B.   formal or designated leadership is unconditional and other members may not per-
form functions equal in importance to or more important than those of the formal
leader
    C.   leadership is a set of learned behaviors
    D.   all of the above

20.   Many constraints in clinical settings must be reckoned with before research can become   20.____
a legitimate and comfortable activity.
However, if nursing is to develop as a research-based practice, it is NOT unreasonable
to expect the nurse in the clinical area to demonstrate

    A.   complete awareness of the process and language of research
    B.   sensitivity to issues related to protecting the rights of human subjects
    C.   an indiscriminate consumption of research findings
    D.   all of the above

21.   Change is the process which leads to alteration in individual or institutional patterns of   21.____
behavior. A nurse can use a number of strategies to implement change.
The three categories described by Bennis, Benne, and Chin do NOT include

    A.   power-coercive   B.   empiric-rational
    C.   situational-demonstrative   D.   all of the above

22.   Nursing research is more than scientific investigation conducted by a person educated   22.____
and credentialed as a nurse.
Diers enumerated three distinguishing properties of nursing research which states that

    A.   the final focus of nursing research must be on a difference that matters in improv-
ing client care

B. nursing research has the potential for contributing to individual patient care
C. a research problem is a nursing research problem when nurses do not have access to or control over the phenomena being studied
D. all of the above

23. Automated client care systems allow *on-line* use of standardized nursing care plans. A specific way in which an automated client care plan can facilitate the role of the nurse does not include that

23.____

A. laboratory data can be ordered by entering a request at a computer workstation
B. the system cannot facilitate complete medications orders
C. the system promotes consistent doctors' orders
D. the use of nursing diagnosis is facilitated because a common format can be used

24. Theory development is considered by many nurses to be one of the most crucial tasks facing the profession today. Three approaches may be used to develop nursing theory including

24.____

A. borrowing conceptual framework from other disciplines and applying them to nursing problems
B. using a reductive approach
C. using a subjective approach
D. all of the above

25. The beliefs underlying a profession are its value system. Generally, these beliefs are similar from model to model and state that

25.____

A. nurses have a unique function even though they share certain functions with other health professionals
B. nursing uses a systematic process to operationalize its conceptual model
C. nursing involves a series of interpersonal relationships
D. all of the above

KEY (CORRECT ANSWERS)

1.	D		11.	B
2.	B		12.	B
3.	C		13.	D
4.	D		14.	A
5.	C		15.	C
6.	A		16.	D
7.	B		17.	C
8.	B		18.	D
9.	C		19.	C
10.	A		20.	B

21.	C
22.	A
23.	B
24.	A
25.	D

EXAMINATION SECTION
TEST 1

DIRECTIONS: Each question or incomplete statement is followed by several suggested answers or completions. Select the one that BEST answers the question or completes the statement. *PRINT THE LETTER OF THE CORRECT ANSWER IN THE SPACE AT THE RIGHT.*

1. A nurse has reached a level of professionalism categorized as *proficient* when he or she   1.____

    A. consciously and deliberately plans nursing care and coordinates complex care demands
    B. recognizes a client's readiness to learn how to manage a treatment program
    C. no longer relies on rules or guidelines
    D. perceives a situation as a whole, rather than just its individual aspects

2. A nurse's separate but interdependent legal roles are generally defined as each of the following EXCEPT   2.____

    A. provider of service
    B. citizen
    C. guardian
    D. employee or contractor for service

3. Administrative law is written within the scope of the authority granted by the   3.____

    A. long-term care facility   B. hospital
    C. legislative body   D. school of nursing

4. In 1992, the American Organization of Nursing Executives published its recommendations for effective health care reform in the United States. Which of the following was NOT an element of these recommendations?   4.____

    A. Finance health care through an increasing reliance on public-sector funding
    B. Increase health care access by the use of physician and non-physician providers
    C. Make provisions for catastrophic care, with some limitation on extraordinary procedures
    D. Encourage consumer partnerships

5. What is the term for the ongoing process of behaving in ways that lead to improved health, or a subjective perception of balance, harmony, and vitality?   5.____

    A. Yin   B. Wellness
    C. Soundness   D. Fitness

6. The *adaptive* model of nursing was developed by   6.____

    A. Watson   B. Roy
    C. Parse   D. Nightingale

7. The voluntary practice of establishing that an individual nurse has met his/her minimum standards of nursing competence in specialized areas is known as   7.____

    A. licensing   B. registration
    C. credentialing   D. certification

8. According to Peplau, the first phase to develop in a nurse-patient relationship is 8.____

    A. resolution   B. identification
    C. orientation   D. exploitation

9. The purpose of a nurse's professional code of ethics is, in its most general sense, to 9.____

    A. provide standards of conduct for the practice of nursing
    B. provide a tool for interpretation of individual expectations
    C. clearly govern the practice of nursing
    D. state the specific decision-making steps in an ethical dilemma

10. A rehabilitation process typically has each of the following broad objectives EXCEPT to 10.____

    A. assist the client to use his or her abilities
    B. return affected abilities to the highest possible level of function
    C. strengthen existing abilities in order to compensate for the loss of others
    D. prevent further disability

11. Persons who perform emergency care in a reasonable and prudent manner, without 11.____
appropriate equipment and supplies, are protected from legal action in most states by

    A. common law   B. Good Samaritan laws
    C. liability insurance   D. nursing practice acts

12. The central concept of _____ is improving or maintaining the quality of life, rather than 12.____
saving life or curing illness.

    A. the health maintenance organization (HMO)
    B. an independent practice association
    C. hospice services
    D. rehabilitation services

13. The purpose of conscience clauses in state abortion legislation is to 13.____

    A. allow medical professionals to refuse participation in third-trimester abortions only
    B. grant hospitals the right to deny admission to abortion clients
    C. implement the federal *gag rule* in hospitals or counseling services about the mention of abortion as an available option
    D. permit nurses or other medical staff to inform patients of their moral obligation to certain procedures

14. Each of the following is true of intentional torts EXCEPT 14.____

    A. the act in question is willful and deliberate
    B. the wrong results from failure to use due care
    C. they involve the commission of a prohibited act
    D. they involve certain specific types of conduct listed as *wrong*

15. In which of the following states would a nursing program use the term *vocational nursing* 15.____
instead of *practical nursing*?

    A. California   B. New York
    C. Illinois   D. Hawaii

16. Which of the following modes of nursing care was developed in response to the shortage of personnel experienced in World War II?

    A. Team nursing
    B. The case method
    C. The functional method
    D. Primary nursing

16.____

17. Most jurisdictions in the United States have statutes that impose a duty on health care professionals to report certain confidential information. Which of the following is NOT a type of information generally included in these statutes?

    A. Vital statistics
    B. Child or elder abuse
    C. Requested medication
    D. Violent incidents

17.____

18. In most states, advanced directives

    A. must be witnessed by at least one person
    B. must be witnessed by two people but do not require review by attorney
    C. may be challenged by members of the client's family
    D. must under all circumstances be reviewed by an attorney

18.____

19. The changing nature of the American health care system has involved many implications for nursing practice. Which of the following is NOT one of these?

    A. Greater demand for assessment and evaluation skills
    B. Demand for researching the cost of nursing care in relation to DRG categories
    C. Greater ability to adapt to a more corporate structure
    D. Decreased need for nurses to function in primary care

19.____

20. Nursing interventions that are based on the instructions or written orders of another professional are classified as

    A. dependent
    B. interdependent
    C. released
    D. independent

20.____

21. A _____ can, under certain circumstances, provide informed consent.

    A. minor
    B. person who is unconscious
    C. client who is sedated and disoriented
    D. mentally ill person who has been judged to be incompetent

21.____

22. Which of the following organizations receives and manages funds and trusts that contribute to the advancement of nursing?

    A. International Council of Nurses (ICN)
    B. American Nursing Association (ANA)
    C. National Federation of Licensed Practical Nurses (NFLPN)
    D. National League for Nursing (NLN)

22.____

23. Which of the following is NOT an example of a primary health care service?

    A. Illness prevention programs
    B. Referring clients to specialists
    C. Restoring clients to useful function in some or all areas of their lives
    D. Explaining a client's overall health problem

23.____

24. A health care professional's duty to do no harm is known as the principle of   24.____

    A. nonmaleficence   B. autonomy
    C. beneficence   D. justice

25. The legal term for touching another's body without consent is   25.____

    A. assault   B. molestation
    C. battery   D. malicious wounding

KEY (CORRECT ANSWERS)

1.	D		11.	B
2.	C		12.	C
3.	C		13.	B
4.	A		14.	B
5.	B		15.	A
6.	B		16.	C
7.	D		17.	C
8.	C		18.	B
9.	A		19.	D
10.	C		20.	A

21. A
22. A
23. C
24. A
25. C

TEST 2

DIRECTIONS: Each question or incomplete statement is followed by several suggested answers or completions. Select the one that BEST answers the question or completes the statement. *PRINT THE LETTER OF THE CORRECT ANSWER IN THE SPACE AT THE RIGHT.*

1. The MAIN difference between a Preferred Provider Organization (PPO) and a Preferred Provider Arrangement (PPA) involves

    A. prepaid premiums
    B. whether services are offered to the insurer at a discounted rate
    C. the degree to which a copayment is applied to services
    D. whether a contract is made with individual providers or an organization of providers

1.____

2. The term for a mental image or classification of things and events in terms of similarities is

    A. framework   B. concept   C. model   D. theory

2.____

3. Which of the following is NOT a type of advanced medical directive?

    A. Durable power of attorney
    B. Living will
    C. Power of executor
    D. Health care proxy

3.____

4. A patient has signed a consent for a perineal surgical procedure. Consent will be most clearly indicated by the patient's statement that

    A. he understands but does not know exactly what will be done during the procedure
    B. his wife wants him to go through with the procedure
    C. he understands the stoma may be permanent
    D. he is in so much pain, he'll sign anything

4.____

5. By the end of the nineteenth century, there were three nursing schools established in the United States. Which of the following was NOT one of these?

    A. Connecticut Training School
    B. Bellevue Hospital School of Nursing
    C. Johns Hopkins School of Nursing
    D. Boston Training School

5.____

6. Nursing _____ is the term for the way in which nursing knowledge is expressed by a practitioner.

    A. ethics   B. science   C. theory   D. esthetics

6.____

7. The time period of a civil litigation procedure is LEAST likely to be affected by

    A. whether an injury or death is involved
    B. the attorneys for both sides
    C. the severity of the complaint
    D. the backlog of cases pending before the court

7.____

8. Which of the following is a characteristic that most clearly distinguishes a profession from other kinds of occupations?

    A. A code of ethics
    B. A complex, sophisticated research apparatus devoted to the enlargement of the body of knowledge pertinent to the role to be performed
    C. The esteem with which members of a society's general population regard the occupation
    D. Its requirement of prolonged specialized training to acquire a body of knowledge pertinent to the role to be performed

8.____

9. _____ is covered under Medicare.

    A. Dentures
    B. Examinations to prescribe eyeglasses
    C. Examinations to prescribe and fit hearing aids
    D. Dental care

9.____

10. The giving of nursing care is an element of the _____ phase of the nursing process.

    A. implementing
    B. assessing
    C. diagnosing
    D. evaluating

10.____

11. Of the following, the first to offer a definition of *nursing process* was

    A. King   B. Travelbee   C. Abdellah   D. Henderson

11.____

12. What type of nursing research has proven to be most difficult to carry out in hospital settings?

    A. Nonexperimental
    B. Experimental
    C. Qualitative
    D. Historical

12.____

13. Each of the following is a general approach to moral theory involved in medical practice EXCEPT

    A. teleology
    B. bioethics
    C. intuitionism
    D. deontology

13.____

14. _____ is a system in which one nurse is responsible for total care of a number of clients 24 hours a day, seven days a week.

    A. Team nursing
    B. Case-method
    C. Functional-method
    D. Primary nursing

14.____

15. The purpose of the prospective payment system (PPS) legislation passed by the federal government in 1983 was *primarily* to

    A. create diagnostic categories for reimbursement
    B. limit the amount of money paid to hospitals that are reimbursed by Medicare
    C. fix the amount of coinsurance for Medicare clients
    D. establish a means of determining reimbursements to providers

15.____

16. When performing aggregation, a nurse's FIRST step is to

    A. establish relationships
    B. conduct nursing research

16.____

C.   collect and summarize clinical interventions
D.   develop nursing theory

17.   The most common malpractice situations involved in nursing care are   17.____

A.   not giving proper attention to patient complaints
B.   medication errors
C.   client falls
D.   mistaken identity

18.   A patient's health records are   18.____

A.   owned by the patient, who always has a right to see them
B.   confidential information that can never be taken to court
C.   concise legal records of all care given and responses
D.   not used by anyone but direct care providers

19.   Each of the following is a service or agency that has been added to some hospitals as a   19.____
result of the changing nature of the health care delivery system EXCEPT

A.   hospice services   B.   nutrition classes
C.   elderly day care   D.   fitness classes

20.   An LPN is working as a staff member at a nursing home. One of the patients, Mr. Thomp-   20.____
son, a 90-year-old, is restless and has spent the last few nights wandering about, unable
to sleep. The LPN is told in report by Ms. Barkley, a fellow nurse, that Ms. Barkley bor-
rowed a Darvocet from another patient and gave it to Mr. Thompson to calm him down.
After the LPN discusses the problem with Ms. Barkley and reports the error to the physician, the next appropriate action would be to

A.   call her attorney to file a complaint
B.   bring the issue to the organization's ethics committee
C.   report the problem to the State Department of Health
D.   do nothing, since an oral reprimand was given

21.   The regulation of nursing is a function of   21.____

A.   the ICN   B.   the ANA
C.   state law   D.   federal law

22.   In order to resolve ethical dilemmas, a nursing staff should establish a sound database   22.____
that will address each of the following questions EXCEPT:

A.   What is the patient's religious affiliation?
B.   What is the intent of the proposed action?
C.   What persons are involved in the situation?
D.   What are the possible consequences of the proposed action?

23.   In 1914,   23.____

A.   the Thompson Practical Nursing School was founded in Brattleboro, Vermont
B.   the association of Practical Nursing Schools was founded

C. the Mississippi State Legislature was the first political body to pass license laws controlling practical nurses

D. Galen Health Institutes, Inc. opened practical/ vocational nursing programs in several states

24. When collecting data during the nursing process, a tertiary source of data would be   24.____

    A. the patient himself
    B. the patient's record
    C. data from family and friends of the patient
    D. the nurse's observations

25. Which of the following is an example of public law affecting nurses?   25.____

    A. Sexual assault
    B. Americans with Disabilities Act
    C. Malpractice
    D. Living wills

KEY (CORRECT ANSWERS)

1.	D	11.	A
2.	B	12.	B
3.	C	13.	B
4.	C	14.	D
5.	C	15.	B
6.	D	16.	C
7.	B	17.	B
8.	D	18.	C
9.	B	19.	A
10.	A	20.	B

21.	C
22.	A
23.	C
24.	B
25.	A

TEST 3

DIRECTIONS: Each question or incomplete statement is followed by several suggested answers or completions. Select the one that BEST answers the question or completes the statement. *PRINT THE LETTER OF THE CORRECT ANSWER IN THE SPACE AT THE RIGHT.*

1. The CHIEF goal of a nurse in the role of care provider is to   1.____

    A. execute planned nursing interventions
    B. convey understanding of about what is important, and to provide support
    C. help the client to recognize and cope with stressful psychological or social problems
    D. prevent illness

2. Each of the following is characteristic of the process for developing critical pathways in a   2.____
medical care facility EXCEPT

    A. a consensus is developed around the management of the case type by a multidisciplinary team that includes physicians
    B. information used includes insurance reimbursements
    C. before it becomes policy, a pathway is piloted in a clinical setting
    D. the process for developing a pathway is created independent of the agency

3. For legal purposes, the standards of care for nursing practice are most clearly defined by   3.____
the

    A. NLN's Standards of Care
    B. ICN's Code of Ethics
    C. ANA's Code for Nurses
    D. state nurse practice act

4. Which of the following is a typical research function of a nurse at the associate degree   4.____
level?

    A. Using nursing practice as a means of gathering data to refine and extend practice
    B. Reading, interpreting, and evaluating research for applicability to nursing practice
    C. Sharing research findings with colleagues
    D. Assisting in data collection within an established, structured format

5. According to the International Council of Nurses, the nurse's fundamental ethical respon-   5.____
sibilities include the following EXCEPT to

    A. prevent illness
    B. sustain a cooperative relationship
    C. restore health
    D. alleviate suffering

6. A nurse who demonstrates marginally accepted performance is professionally catego-   6.____
rized as

    A. a novice   B. an advanced beginner
    C. competent   D. proficient

7. A resident physician instructs nurses to order a complete blood count and urinalysis on   7.____
all clients admitted to the emergency room and to get the results before calling him
down. The nurses feel this is unethical; it is wasteful and causes discomfort and possible
risks for the clients. Without having the authority to change the situation, however, they
order the tests, feel guilty, and upset. This is an example of

    A. a decision-focused ethical problem
    B. an action-focused ethical problem
    C. intuitionism
    D. a deontological ethical problem

8. Each of the following has contributed to the professional nurse's increased role as a   8.____
teacher EXCEPT

    A. new emphasis on health promotion
    B. increased client awareness
    C. shortened hospital stays
    D. increase in long-term illnesses and disabilities

9. According to Miller, the critical aspects of professionalism in nursing do NOT include   9.____

    A. delineating and specifying the skills and competencies that are the boundaries of
       expertise
    B. attaining a competence derived from the theoretical base
    C. gaining a body of knowledge in a university setting
    D. gaining a science orientation at the hospital level in nursing

10. When the American Society of Superintendents of Training Schools of Nursing was   10.____
established in 1894, its primary goal was

    A. to promote the establishment of nursing education programs throughout the United
       States
    B. the increase in prestige and remuneration of civil nursing practice as compared to
       wartime nursing
    C. the establishment of educational standards for nursing
    D. recruitment and training of qualified nursing personnel

11. The general term for an expected standard of behavior for specific group members is   11.____

    A. folkway   B. law   C. rule   D. norm

12. It is NOT a purpose of nursing codes of ethics to   12.____

    A. give direction for actions to take in specific cases
    B. remind nurses of the special responsibility they assume when caring for the sick
    C. provide a sign of the profession's commitment to the public it serves
    D. guide the profession in self-regulation

13. _____ stimuli are most immediate to a patient, and precipitate certain observed behav-   13.____
iors.

    A. Focal   B. Contextual
    C. Residual   D. Primary

14. Since 1965, health care costs in the United States have increased by approximately   14._____

    A.   100%   B.   200%   C.   400%   D.   600%

15. Before a civil trial, written answers to written questions, known as _____, are submitted   15._____
by all parties.

    A.   discoveries   B.   depositions
    C.   affidavits   D.   interrogatories

16. In what year were the Medicare amendments to the Social Security Act adopted?   16._____

    A.   1945   B.   1955   C.   1965   D.   1975

17. Which of the following is a type of therapeutic intervention?   17._____

    A.   Educating   B.   Monitoring
    C.   Inspecting   D.   Observing

18. Which of the following is NOT typically involved in a nurse's responsibility as witness to a   18._____
client's informed consent?

    A.   Witnessing the client's signature
    B.   Witnessing the exchange between the client and the physician
    C.   Establishing that the client fully understands
    D.   Securing the approval of a patient's living relation

19. Of the following, which patient value is most threatened by health care situations?   19._____

    A.   Equity   B.   Security   C.   Autonomy   D.   Well-being

20. Which of the following is a secondary health care agency?   20._____

    A.   Hospice   B.   Crisis center
    C.   Long-term care facility   D.   Hospital

21. Which of the following is NOT an important priority of data collection during the assess-   21._____
ment phase of the nursing process?

    A.   Communicating with the client, rather than consulting secondary sources
    B.   Including information about both strengths and needs
    C.   Arranging results in a way easily retrievable by future researchers
    D.   Including the client's responses to current alterations

22. Which of the following was the creator of nursing's *four conservation principles*?   22._____

    A.   Neuman   B.   Orem   C.   Levine   D.   Rogers

23. Which of the following is not an essential element of nursing diagnosis?   23._____

    A.   Focusing on person's responses
    B.   Labeling conclusions
    C.   Suggesting interventions
    D.   Representing an opinion

24. Each of the following is a recommendation offered by the ANA regarding *do not resusci-   24.____
    tate* (DNR) orders EXCEPT

    A. the wishes of the client's spouse and family must always take precedence
    B. when the client is incompetent, an advance directive or the surrogate decision-
        makers should make treatment decisions
    C. if it is contrary to the nurse's personal beliefs to carry out a DNR order, the nurse
        should consult the nursing manager for a change in assignment
    D. a DNR order is separate from other aspects of a client's care, and does not imply
        that other types of care should be withdrawn

25. The scientific method is useful in nursing research for   25.____

    A. applying research principles into real-world practice
    B. overcoming current inabilities to measure most concepts of interest to nurses
    C. to find answers to clinical problems
    D. helping to answer ethical or value questions

KEY (CORRECT ANSWERS)

1.	B	11.	D
2.	D	12.	A
3.	D	13.	A
4.	D	14.	C
5.	B	15.	D
6.	B	16.	C
7.	B	17.	A
8.	B	18.	D
9.	D	19.	C
10.	C	20.	D

21.	C
22.	C
23.	D
24.	A
25.	C

EXAMINATION SECTION
TEST 1

DIRECTIONS: Each question or incomplete statement is followed by several suggested answers or completions. Select the one that BEST answers the question or completes the statement. *PRINT THE LETTER OF THE CORRECT ANSWER IN THE SPACE AT THE RIGHT.*

Questions 1-6.

DIRECTIONS: Questions 1 through 6 are to be answered on the basis of the following information.

The nursing staff on a medical unit meets every week to discuss problem areas they are encountering while giving nursing care. The areas of discussion are (1) the nursing process and (2) emotional needs of clients.

1. The first staff meeting covers the best nursing approach to meet the clients' emotional needs.
    Which basic factor should be determined FIRST by the staff?   1._____

    A.   Why the clients behave as they do
    B.   Which nursing approach has been effective or needs changing
    C.   Which clients have symptoms of increased anxiety
    D.   What dependent needs of the client the nurse can meet

2. The staff discusses methods of data collection by the nurse.   2._____
    Which would be the MOST significant in making a nursing care plan?

    A.   The nursing report on the client's problems
    B.   The physical/emotional history supplied by the client's family
    C.   Reviewing the client's chart
    D.   Interviewing the client immediately on admission

3. The staff agrees that the BASIC principle of planning nursing care is to   3._____

    A.   accept the client as he or she is
    B.   meet the client's needs
    C.   believe the client will improve
    D.   know the client as a person

4. The staff also stresses that, at the initial interview with the client, the nurse should use   4._____
    open-ended questions to collect data.
    Which question would be a good example?

    A.   Are there any questions you want to ask?
    B.   Tell me something about yourself.
    C.   Can you give me any information?
    D.   Were you brought to the hospital by your family?

5. The nursing staff discusses evaluation of nursing care. Which evaluation should be identified as a *halo* evaluation? The client('s)   5.____

    A. has learned some control
    B. behavior is to demand attention
    C. continues to be negative
    D. care plan has been effective

6. The staff identifies the best time for the nurse to record the observed behavior of a client.   6.____
That time is

    A. when the behavior has become a problem
    B. at the end of every shift
    C. immediately after contact with the client
    D. after conferring with other staff members

7. Many people with mental disorders have poor self-images, which they need to improve in   7.____
order to recover.
All of the following factors contribute to self-image EXCEPT

    A. body image
    B. personally judging others
    C. relationships within the family
    D. interpersonal relationships outside of the family

8. The MOST important feeling for the nurse to convey to the client in order for the client to   8.____
accept the nurse is one of

    A. respect for the client   B. willingness to help
    C. professional competence   D. no-nonsense demands

9. A patient being treated for an aggressive personality disorder insists that the last time he   9.____
was in the clinic he was given lithium, which helped him, and he demands that the nurse
get him some immediately.
The nurse's BEST reply to this demand would be:

    A. We never administer drugs to people in your condition
    B. I will go get some for you if you calm down
    C. You don't need lithium
    D. Be patient, and I'll talk to your doctor about whether lithium would be appropriate
       for you

10. All of the following principles of psychiatric-mental health nursing help form the basis of   10.____
the therapeutic use of self EXCEPT:

    A. Be aware of your own feelings and responses and maintain objectivity while being
       aware of your own needs
    B. Accept clients as they are, be nonjudgmental, and recognize that emotions influ-
       ence behaviors
    C. Use sympathy, not empathy, and observe a client's behaviors to analyze needs and
       problems
    D. Avoid verbal reprimands, physical force, giving advice, or imposing your own val-
       ues on clients. Also assess clients in the context of their social and cultural group.

Questions 11-20.

DIRECTIONS: Questions 11 through 20 are to be answered on the basis of the following information.

Pete Jones, the mental health nurse specialist, conducts group therapy sessions for the outpatient clinic.

11. During group formation, Mr. Jones should SPECIFICALLY select a group of clients that is no more than _____ in number and has homogeneity of _____.   11.____

    A. 6; goals
    B. 4; age and sex
    C. 14; ability and willingness
    D. 10; problems and needs

12. Mr. Jones has selected his group, and they meet daily from 2 to 3 P.M. It is a closed group and does not allow any interruptions.   12.____
During the period that it takes the group to become acquainted, what kind of behavior would Mr. Jones expect from the group?

    A. Open and positive interaction, rather than projection of their feelings
    B. Conflict, lack of unity, testing, and politeness toward each other
    C. Trust and acceptance of each other and the therapist
    D. Discussion centering on the mental health unit and their expectations

13. Mr. Jones explains to the group that its main function is sharing feelings and behaviors among the members. The group is often a substitute for, or is compared to, one's own family.   13.____
What does the group accomplish for each member through this identification process?
The group

    A. gives the client hope in himself and makes him realize that others are available for comfort and acceptance
    B. teaches the client new skills in socialization that will be more acceptable to his family
    C. assists the client in replacing negative past experiences with a new set of positive group experiences
    D. helps the client feel that he is being helpful and interested in the well-being of others

14. Mr. Jones' group therapy is based on interventive-exploratory therapy.   14.____
When he defines this type of therapy to his group, what should he say?

    A. You will verbally express your emotional problems with individual and group relationships.
    B. The main focus of this group is the support of existing coping mechanisms.
    C. The emphasis is on social interaction, which encourages control.
    D. This is an intellectual and emotional exchange of things that you value.

15. Mr. Jones observes that one of the clients monopolizes the group discussion. 15.____
What action should Mr. Jones take?

    A. Accept the client's behavior as his/her way of coping
    B. Allow the group members to intervene if they are able to
    C. Interrupt and ask the client to limit the discussion
    D. Ask another client if this discussion is relevant

16. One of the clients in the group is verbally aggressive toward another client. 16.____
What should Mr. Jones do INITIALLY?

    A. Set up individual therapy to explore the hostile client's feelings
    B. Ask the aggressive client to leave the group until control is gained
    C. Set an example by being uninvolved with the aggressor
    D. Sit still, observe, and avoid taking sides with either client

17. Mr. Jones and the group feel that they are not progressing. What should the group do? 17.____

    A. Explore the reasons for the lack of group productivity
    B. Establish other goals that will be more compatible to the group
    C. Disband because the members are not compatible
    D. Accept new members into the group to provide more feedback

18. After a group session, one of the clients says, *Today I felt we were really a group.* 18.____
When Mr. Jones asks that client to identify the reason for this feeling, which response
demonstrates ACCURATELY that the group was cohesive?

    A. We have learned to speak directly to each other rather than to the whole group.
    B. We have been able to discuss similarities of thoughts and conflicts.
    C. We have not been so hostile or anxious with each other.
    D. As individuals, each one has identified ways of fulfilling his or her goal.

19. During one of the group sessions, Mrs. Elena tells Mr. Jones that he is one of the smart- 19.____
est men she has ever known and feels she has learned so much from him.
How should Mr. Jones respond?

    A. That is very nice of you, but we are not here to discuss me.
    B. We are not here to give compliments to any one member.
    C. You seem anxious, share your feelings with us.
    D. The purpose of the group is to learn more about each other.

20. The group has reached its goal and is now talking about termination. 20.____
Which action by the group members shows that they are ready to terminate the group?

    A. Members no longer feel abandoned, rejected, or forsaken.
    B. Feelings are expressed that members of the group will keep in touch.
    C. Each member learns to handle his or her own feelings of loss without support.
    D. There is effective coping with feelings of loss and separation anxiety.

———

KEY (CORRECT ANSWERS)

1.	C	11.	D
2.	D	12.	B
3.	A	13.	C
4.	B	14.	A
5.	C	15.	B
6.	C	16.	D
7.	B	17.	A
8.	A	18.	B
9.	D	19.	C
10.	C	20.	D

TEST 2

DIRECTIONS: Each question or incomplete statement is followed by several suggested answers or completions. Select the one that BEST answers the question or completes the statement. *PRINT THE LETTER OF THE CORRECT ANSWER IN THE SPACE AT THE RIGHT.*

Questions 1-6.

DIRECTIONS: Questions 1 through 6 are to be answered on the basis of the following information.

Ms. Cohen is a nurse working in a crisis center with a volunteer group.

1. One of the volunteers asks, *What is a crisis?* The nurse should reply that a crisis is a situation in which the person or family

   A. is too subjectively involved to realize when there is a problem
   B. constantly looks to others to resolve certain conflicts
   C. has difficulty with growth and development periods
   D. has had no experience in knowing how to deal with a problem

1.____

2. Ms. Cohen tells the volunteers that those working with people in crisis should recognize that one of the first reactions to crisis is the use of defense mechanisms. They should know that these defenses at the time of a crisis

   A. are useful in helping clients protect themselves
   B. are irrelevant, as they are part of the basic personality
   C. should be interrupted to prevent further damage
   D. are an indication that the client is coping well

2.____

3. Ms. Cohen explains to the group that people in crisis often use isolation as a defense. Ms. Cohen asks, *Which behavior should be assessed as isolation?*
   The person

   A. blames others for causing the problem
   B. minimizes the seriousness of the problem
   C. accepts the problem intellectually but not emotionally
   D. puts excess energy in another area to neutralize the problem

3.____

4. Ms. Cohen instructs the volunteers that when people in crisis first come to the center to seek information about their problem, only specific questions should be answered, with no details given at this time.
   Why is this approach taken?

   A. The person may be mentally incompetent and may lose control.
   B. A nurse or doctor should give specific information.
   C. The person may be overwhelmed with excessive information.
   D. The person is not interested in detailed information.

4.____

54

5. Ms. Cohen states that when a person is in crisis, the BEST support group would be   5.____

    A. the volunteers in the community
    B. close family and friends understanding the problem
    C. other people who have similar problems
    D. the professional working in the crisis center

6. One of the volunteers asks, *Why is the crisis intervention limited from 1 to 6 weeks?*   6.____
Ms. Cohen replies that a person can stand the disequilibrium only for a limited time, and during this time will

    A. more likely accept intervention to help with coping
    B. return to a familiar pattern of behavior
    C. require long-term counseling after this period
    D. refuse help from any other support group

Questions 7-11.

DIRECTIONS: Questions 7 through 11 are to be answered on the basis of the following information.

Lauren Oland, age 14, was brought to the crisis center by a policeman. She had been raped by a friend of the family.

7. Which nursing action should have TOP priority?   7.____

    A. Explain to her that she will be safe here.
    B. Get a detailed description of the attack.
    C. Have a calm and accepting approach.
    D. Treat her physical wounds.

8. Lauren Oland sobs, *My family will kill me if they find out.* Which response by the nurse   8.____
would be MOST appropriate?

    A. You are underage so your family will have to be informed.
    B. Your family is your best support at this time.
    C. Don't you think that they would rather kill the man?
    D. Tell me how your family reacts during stressful times.

9. After Lauren calms down and accepts Ms. Cohen, she confides, *I feel so dirty. I will never*   9.____
feel clean again. How should the nurse reply?

    A. This is a normal feeling after what has happened to you.
    B. Are you saying you feel guilty? Let's talk about that feeling.
    C. I can understand; I would feel the same way.
    D. You shouldn't think of yourself as dirty; it wasn't your fault.

10. Lauren tells the nurse, *I feel like my love life is over. No decent boy will ever look at me*   10.____
again.
To help Lauren assess the situation, how should the nurse reply?

    A. I know it is difficult, but you are strong.
    B. You are not to blame so you shouldn't punish yourself.

C. What was your relationship with boys before?
D. You are a pretty girl; you will have many boyfriends.

11. Lauren tells Ms. Cohen that she will not testify against the family friend because then everyone will know about her.
Which reply by the nurse would BEST help Lauren with this plan of action?

    A. How do you think you will feel if you do nothing?
    B. It will be a closed court, so no one will know.
    C. This is difficult, but I'm sure you will make the right choice.
    D. You have an obligation to protect other women from this man.

11.____

Questions 12-15.

DIRECTIONS: Questions 12 through 15 are to be answered on the basis of the following information.

Kirt Russel, a volunteer, answers the hotline. The caller, a female, tells Kirt that she plans on killing herself.

12. How should Kirt reply?

    A. Are you alone? Is there someone else that I can talk to?
    B. How do you plan on killing yourself?
    C. You have called the right number to prevent that from happening.
    D. What is your name, address, and telephone number?

12.____

13. What is the BEST approach for Kirt to take while talking to the *suicide caller*?

    A. Neutral, not condoning or condemning
    B. Distracting the caller from talking about suicide
    C. One of concern and support
    D. Acting as the conscience of the caller

13.____

14. The caller identifies herself as Barbra and states that she is going to poison herself. What should Kirt then say?

    A. Have you thought of the agony of such a death?
    B. What kind of poison are you going to take?
    C. Tell me if you've ever had these feelings before.
    D. Give me the name of your doctor.

14.____

15. Kirt keeps Barbra on the phone, pleading with her not to hang up, but to keep talking to him.
Kirt's purpose in doing this is to

    A. give her time to gain her equilibrium and reconsider her actions
    B. let her know that someone cares enough to talk to her
    C. keep her mind off her problems and the thought of suicide
    D. keep her occupied until an emergency team arrives

15.____

Questions 16-20.

DIRECTIONS: Questions 16 through 20 are to be answered on the basis of the following information.

Doreen Darby is a 16-year-old high school student with a history of poor social contact.
Always an introvert, for the past month Doreen has refused to go to school, spent her time in
bed, and taken nourishment only when spoon-fed. Her family took her to the emergency room
of the general hospital when she reported that voices had told her she was *no good and
should stay away from others.*

16. The nurse in the emergency room identifies Doreen's behavior as depersonalization.   16.____
This term is BEST described as

    A. pathological narcissism
    B. inability to empathize with others
    C. experiencing the world as dreamlike
    D. absence of a moral code

17. The staff is planning Doreen's immediate care. The MOST suitable choice at this time   17.____
would be

    A. weekly visits to the psychiatric clinic for medical therapy and psychotherapy
    B. a small psychiatric unit for 24 hour-a-day treatment
    C. attendance at the day hospital and home with her family at night
    D. in her home, with her family, under the supervision of a psychiatrist

18. Doreen is assessed as having low self-esteem. Which characteristic BEST defines this   18.____
problem?

    A. Social withdrawal   B. Flat faces
    C. Alienation from self   D. Feelings of persecution

19. The nursing staff plans an intensive therapeutic approach for Doreen.   19.____
Such an approach is CRUCIAL for Doreen because

    A. she will be missing her family, which is her primary support group
    B. she is acutely ill and is completely out of contact with reality
    C. the staff must thoroughly evaluate Doreen's physical, social, and emotional condi-
tion
    D. it is critical for her to learn to trust those in her environment

20. Doreen has learned to relate to her primary nurse but refuses to get involved in any of   20.____
the activities with others on the unit.
Which approach by her primary nurse would be the MOST therapeutic for Doreen?

    A. Telling Doreen she is expected at assigned activities
    B. Becoming involved in activities with Doreen
    C. Observing Doreen with others
    D. Waiting until Doreen asks to attend the activities

Questions 21-25.

DIRECTIONS: Questions 21 through 25 are to be answered on the basis of the following information.

Mrs. Agnes Smith comes to the crisis center with her two small daughters, ages 3 and 4. She has numerous contusions on her face and body. She tells the nurse, *I've been beaten by my husband for the last time. I want to leave him but have no place to go. Maybe when he sobers up, I can go back - if he will go on the wagon.*

21. Which analysis by the nurse takes PRIORITY?　　　　　　　　　　21.____

    A. Recognize that the client is correct in wanting to leave her husband
    B. Know the effect the problem will have on the client
    C. Use own past experience to help the client understand her problem
    D. Understand the implications of the problem from the client's viewpoint

22. During the assessment period, which question should the nurse ask Mrs. Smith?　　22.____

    A. Why can't you plan to live with your family?
    B. Does your husband earn enough to support two households?
    C. How often does your husband beat you?
    D. You say you want to go yet stay. Are there any alternatives we can discuss?

23. Mrs. Smith has identified her problem as being too dependent on her husband. What plan would BEST help her resolve this problem?　　23.____

    A. Learn to have a better self-image
    B. Talk to her husband about her need to be independent
    C. Find a new home for herself and her children
    D. Go to school or get a job

24. The children and Mrs. Smith have made contact with friends and will be temporarily staying with them.　　24.____
The nurse understands that this is important for the family at this time because

    A. the tension in their own home is too great
    B. in a neutral environment Mrs. Smith can better plan for the future
    C. they will be safer there than in their own home
    D. both the abuser and abused need time apart

25. Mrs. Smith plans to go to group therapy. Which group would be MOST beneficial at this time?　　25.____

    A. Abusers Anonymous
    B. Family therapy
    C. Parents without partners
    D. Al-Anon

KEY (CORRECT ANSWERS)

1.	D		11.	A
2.	A		12.	D
3.	C		13.	C
4.	C		14.	B
5.	B		15.	D
6.	A		16.	C
7.	C		17.	B
8.	D		18.	A
9.	B		19.	D
10.	C		20.	B

21.	D
22.	D
23.	A
24.	C
25.	B

———

EXAMINATION SECTION
TEST 1

DIRECTIONS: Each question or incomplete statement is followed by several suggested answers or completions. Select the one that BEST answers the question or completes the statement. *PRINT THE LETTER OF THE CORRECT ANSWER IN THE SPACE AT THE RIGHT.*

1. The word *supervision* is subject to many interpretations, depending on the area in which it functions.
   Of the following, the statement which represents the BEST definition of supervision as it functions in nursing is that it is a(n)

   A. educational process for the training of personnel
   B. administrative process aimed at economy of performance
   C. leadership process for the development of new leaders
   D. cooperative process for the improvement of service

   1.____

2. Of the following, the one which BEST defines a *philosophy of supervision* in nursing is that it is a(n)

   A. practical application of the principles of public health nursing
   B. general statement of the overall purposes of the supervisory process
   C. unchanging guide based on the functions of the supervisor
   D. adaptation of the principles of public health nursing to the service of a particular agency

   2.____

3. Principles of supervision are generally accepted rules governing the supervisory process.
   They are PRIMARILY important because they

   A. are guides to methods and activities
   B. are standards for evaluating supervision
   C. eliminate the need for *techniques* for nursing performance
   D. reflect administrative policies

   3.____

4. Of the following, the one on which the objectives of a supervisory program in nursing should PRIMARILY be based is

   A. the health problems of the community
   B. a job analysis of supervisory functions
   C. administrative policies of the agency
   D. the needs of the staff nurses

   4.____

5. Certain restrictions on the functions of the supervisor are inherent in the nature of the process of supervision. Of the following statements, the one which will BEST serve as a guide in determining supervisory functions is that

   A. since supervision is educational, the supervisor should require each staff nurse to further her own education through advanced study
   B. the supervisor has some responsibility for social reforms since public health nursing is interested in improving living standards

   5.____

C.   supervision should not extend beyond the point where its influence affects the service program of the agency
D.   the supervisor has some responsibility for the health of the staff nurses and should guide their recreational and social activities

6.   Of the following, the BEST method for a supervisor to use in order to develop the staff nurse's understanding of nursing is to   6.____

A.   encourage all nurses to further their professional growth through advanced study
B.   help the nurses to solve family problems by the use of all community agencies
C.   develop concepts of family and community health through individual supervision of each nurse's work
D.   plan group education programs which will bring in speakers from all kinds of health agencies in the community

7.   Democratic supervision recognizes individual differences and values.   7.____
Of the following statements, the one which represents the BEST interpretation of a democratic approach to the staff nurse is that

A.   each nurse should receive an equal amount of guidance from the supervisor
B.   each nurse has something of value to contribute to the service
C.   staff nurses and supervisors should accept equal responsibility for the work of the agency
D.   the work of each nurse is of equal value to the agency

8.   Changes in public health and nursing practice affect the function of the supervisor in public health nursing.   8.____
Of the following, the one which represents a trend in public health or nursing practice which will affect supervisory functions is that the

A.   intangible nature of present day health guidance increases the need for staff nurses prepared as *specialists* in many areas
B.   public health nurse is expected to function as a partner in the health team
C.   modern public health nurse is expected to function independently
D.   multiplicity of community agencies and health workers has decreased the demands made on public health nurses for participation in community activities

9.   Of the following methods, the one which represents the BEST supervisory practice with regard to scheduling work for nurses is to   9.____

A.   schedule each nurse's work on a daily basis to insure even distribution of work
B.   schedule routine assignments on a monthly basis and special assignments on a daily basis
C.   make scheduling of work a staff responsibility except for relief assignments
D.   make it a cooperative activity for supervisor and staff

10. Assignment of work is one means which may be utilized by the supervisor as a method of staff development.   10.____
Of the following, the principle which it would be BEST to follow in making work assignments, considering the total functions of the supervisor, is to

    A.   plan varying work assignments for the districts so that the needs of each individual nurse can be met

    B.   give primary consideration to the needs of the nurse, since service demands can be distributed among the entire staff

    C.   consider the nurse's ability and potential growth since both the nurse and the service will profit

    D.   discontinue the services of a nurse who cannot carry a routine work assignment in any area

11.   The maintenance of *morale* within the staff group is one of the important responsibilities of the supervisor.
Of the following, the BEST way to strengthen morale in a staff group where dissatisfaction exists because of heavy case loads is to   11.____

    A.   recommend to administration that nurses receive extra compensation for overtime hours on duty

    B.   reduce large case loads by discharging families where only minor problems exist

    C.   present the problem for discussion at a staff meeting and ask for suggested solutions

    D.   rotate work assignments, alternating the heavy and light districts among all the staff

12.   Of the following statements, the one which BEST represents the philosophy of the recommended ratio of supervisors to staff nurses is that   12.____

    A.   the ratio can be reduced when more qualified public health workers are available

    B.   the trend toward employment of non-nurses for some tasks will make it possible to reduce the ratio

    C.   the ratio can be reduced when qualified specialist consultants are available

    D.   since the work of the public health nurse is becoming increasingly more complex, the ratio may need to be increased

13.   Older staff nurses are frequently resistant to new ideas and present a problem to the supervisor.
The BEST approach in handling this situation is to   13.____

    A.   encourage the nurses to take courses which will bring them *up to date*

    B.   avoid situations which tend to generate resistance

    C.   have the nurses assist in conducting activities which include new ideas

    D.   use supervisory authority to request their cooperation

14.   Field observation as a supervisory technique is of *particular* value PRIMARILY because it   14.____

    A.   keeps the supervisor in touch with the realities of the work

    B.   best reveals the strengths and weaknesses of the staff

    C.   is an economical procedure

    D.   gives the supervisor an opportunity to check on the nurse's techniques

15.   An individual conference between supervisor and staff nurse can be considered *successful* if   15.____

    A.   all of the nurse's problems have been discussed
    B.   the nurse accepts all the supervisor's suggestions
    C.   free discussion takes place between supervisor and nurse
    D.   the nurse assumes responsibility for self-evaluation

16.   The development of citizens advisory committees for official health agencies is a definite   16.____
trend in community health organizations.
The PARTICULAR value of such a committee is that it

    A.   develops general citizen interest in community health and community health projects
    B.   encourages the hiring of better prepared personnel
    C.   develops new health programs in accordance with community needs
    D.   provides volunteer service for community health work

17.   Evaluation of the overall performance of the staff nurses as a group is an administrative   17.____
as well as an educational function.
From the *administrative* point of view, it serves as a(n)

    A.   aid to the director in securing the necessary budget
    B.   means of justifying the service
    C.   basis for planning staff education
    D.   basis for setting up job qualifications

18.   Of the following, the one which is the BEST criterion of the success of the supervisor is   18.____
her ability to

    A.   mold the staff nurses into a desirable pattern established by her
    B.   develop the resources of the staff nurses with the maximum degree of efficiency
    C.   secure the consent of the staff nurses to follow established nursing policies
    D.   develop and maintain cooperation between staff and administrative groups

19.   Of the following, the one which would be *irrelevant* in a self-analysis of supervisory effi-   19.____
ciency is:

    A.   Is there evidence of job satisfaction among members of the staff?
    B.   Do vital statistics show a reduction in morbidity and mortality rates in the community?
    C.   Do nurses' case records show an improvement in the type of nursing service rendered?
    D.   Is there evidence of cooperative working relationships with other agencies in the community?

20.   Of the following statements, the one which BEST represents the responsibility of the   20.____
nurse in the community health program is

    A.   planning and putting into action a community-wide health program
    B.   interpreting the public health program to the community
    C.   giving health guidance to families and individuals
    D.   participating in the public relations program of community health agencies

21. When selecting a case load for a new staff nurse during her period of introduction to a public health nursing agency, it is MOST advisable to assign her to

    A. a variety of cases to give her a complete picture of the agency program
    B. cases involving contact with many community agencies to give her a picture of the community
    C. cases with difficult and varied health and social problems to determine her ability to adjust to the work
    D. cases which will give her an opportunity to see the function of a public health nurse in family health service

21._____

22. In evaluating personal qualities which are desirable in nurses, it is important to base judgments on objective behavior.
Of the following statements, the one that describes *objective* behavior is:

    A. Does not show loyalty to the organization
    B. Has made several excellent suggestions for staff conferences
    C. Is well liked by patients and secures their cooperation
    D. Seems incapable of any sustained effort towards improvement

22._____

23. A staff nurse who needs help in planning and organizing her work can BEST be assisted by

    A. encouraging her to analyze her work as a basis for planning
    B. having her keep a careful record of all her activities
    C. having her work scheduled carefully by the supervisor
    D. suggesting that she not plan for more than one day's work at a time

23._____

24. Many facets of the work of the nurse cannot be developed in a short period of introduction to the service.
Of the following, the one which needs *particularly* long time guidance and supervision is for the nurse to

    A. acquire the ability to adjust to the general field of public health nursing
    B. appreciate the dynamic nature of public health nursing
    C. acquire knowledge of the routine techniques required
    D. develop skill in family health teaching

24._____

25. The level of achievement which should be reached by an average staff nurse at the end of a two-month introductory period in a public health nursing agency is

    A. knowledge of the total health program in the community
    B. ability to plan a program of health instruction
    C. ability to accept responsibility for nursing service to a selected number of families
    D. awareness of the chief health problems of the community

25._____

KEY (CORRECT ANSWERS)

1.	D	11.	C
2.	B	12.	D
3.	A	13.	C
4.	A	14.	A
5.	C	15.	C
6.	C	16.	A
7.	B	17.	B
8.	B	18.	B
9.	D	19.	B
10.	C	20.	C

21. D
22. B
23. A
24. D
25. C

―――――

TEST 2

DIRECTIONS: Each question or incomplete statement is followed by several suggested answers or completions. Select the one that BEST answers the question or completes the statement. *PRINT THE LETTER OF THE CORRECT ANSWER IN THE SPACE AT THE RIGHT.*

1. The successful staff education program is one which is carefully planned by the supervi-   1.____
   sor and the staff nurses. Of the following statements, the one which represents the BEST
   basis for planning a staff education program is the

   A. needs of the staff nurses as expressed by the supervisory group
   B. chief health problems of the community
   C. needs of the staff nurses as they are related to the needs of the service
   D. problems in nursing service as seen by the administrator

2. A procedure manual is a supervisory tool which can be of assistance to the nursing   2.____
   supervisor in that it

   A. frees her of the necessity of routine checking of technique
   B. gives her assurance that the staff nurses will give safe nursing care
   C. provides a basis for the necessary standardization of nursing techniques
   D. insures that administrative policies are understood by the staff

3. The staff education program is a major responsibility of the supervisor in a nursing pro-   3.____
   gram. To do an effective job, the supervisor needs a knowledge of the principles that gov-
   ern teaching-learning situations.
   These principles are based PRIMARILY on

   A. psychological factors that operate in the teaching-learning situation
   B. standardized tests
   C. practical experience of teachers
   D. studies made by experts in the field

4. Dramatization of incidents by means of role playing as a technique of staff education is of   4.____
   particular value PRIMARILY because it

   A. helps the nurse to understand patient attitudes
   B. gives the nurse confidence in meeting difficult situations
   C. develops leadership and teaching potentialities
   D. gives the nurse the feeling of true life situations

5. The *particular* value of the case study method of teaching in staff education is to   5.____

   A. give nurses help in solving the problems of the family under discussion
   B. provide training in problem solving by making problem situations more concrete
   C. familiarize the nurse with community agencies which may assist in solving family
      problems
   D. help nurses understand why families do not always cooperate with plans made for
      them

6. Assume that a staff nurse under your supervision is familiar with teaching principles and methods and that her knowledge is adequate, yet she fails to put her teaching across to the families.
Of the following methods, the one which would be BEST for the supervisor to use to help this nurse is to

   A. suggest additional reading references
   B. encourage her to make written teaching plans
   C. give her practice in teaching large groups
   D. assist her in making practical applications in specific cases

6.____

7. The use of special lecturers in staff education has definite value in certain instances. A *specific* value of this method is that it

   A. provides information not readily available in printed form
   B. stimulates group participation in discussion
   C. presents material of a controversial nature
   D. promotes cooperation between agencies

7.____

8. Proper preparation is an important factor for a group discussion and is the responsibility of the discussion leader.
Of the following, the one which does NOT constitute part of the leader's preparation is

   A. preparing an outline for the discussion
   B. assembling the necessary visual aids
   C. providing factual material for the discussants
   D. determining the conclusion he desires

8.____

9. Of the following, the MOST important requirement for a discussion leader is that he

   A. be an *expert* on the subject to be discussed
   B. have the ability to stimulate others to think and to express themselves
   C. have an aggressive personality
   D. have the ability to lead others toward an acceptance of his opinions

9.____

10. Of the following suggested criteria, the one which is MOST valid in judging the success of a group discussion is whether

    A. there were no more than 40 nor fewer than 30 participants
    B. the discussion resulted in complete agreement among the members
    C. all issues were resolved at the close of the discussion
    D. effective and constructive group action resulted from the discussion

10.____

11. Supervision of recording includes various activities, one of which is the routine checking of records.
Of the following, the CHIEF purpose of this type of record review is to

    A. build staff interest in records
    B. promote accuracy and completeness
    C. assure that visits are made on schedule
    D. secure information for use in record revision

11.____

12. Assume that a staff nurse does good work but keeps poor records.   12.____
Of the following, the method which would contribute MOST toward the improvement of her record keeping is to

     A. give her close individual supervision and guidance
     B. assign her to check the records of other staff nurses for inaccuracies
     C. check all her records daily for omissions and errors
     D. make her responsible for a staff education meeting on *Records*

13. A staff nurse constantly meets resistance from families in attempting to secure informa-   13.____
tion for records.
Of the following, it would be MOST advisable for the supervisor to suggest to the staff nurse that she

     A. defer asking for information for records until she knows the families and is accepted by them
     B. try getting the required information without letting the families know that it is going to be recorded
     C. let the families see the record and assist the nurse in filling it out
     D. explain to the families the need of the information and that it is kept confidential

14. Leadership is an important technique in the supervisory process.   14.____
Of the following characteristics, the one which would provide for the BEST kind of leadership in nursing is

     A. aggressiveness in attacking problems
     B. confidence in one's ability to lead others
     C. a dynamic, extrovert type of personality
     D. ability to inspire confidence in others

15. Field experience for university students in public health nursing programs provides an   15.____
opportunity for the integration of theory with practic The agency is not expected to duplicate material covered in the classroom, but to develop it.
Of the following, the one for which the university has the *right* to expect the field agency to accept PRIMARY responsibility is

     A. developing the nurse's ability to plan teaching
     B. having the nurse understand the purposes and functions of records
     C. helping the nurse to recognize and appreciate teaching opportunities
     D. teaching the nurse to understand the psychological basis of teaching and learning

16. If the shortage of public health nurses continues, agencies giving services will be   16.____
required to make adjustments in their programs. Decisions will have to be made as to which services are essential and which can be cut to a minimum or discontinued.
Of the following services, the one which under these circumstances could be *curtailed* is home visits to

     A. give bedside care in acute illness
     B. tuberculosis patients and their families
     C. mothers and newborn babies delivered in the hospitals
     D. patients under adequate treatment for syphilis

17. The use of time studies is a method which the nursing supervisor may use to advantage   17.____
in self-evaluation. Of the following information secured as a result of a time study made
by a supervisor, the one which would be an *indication* of the need for better work planning and organization is that there has been a(n)

    A. *increase* in the time spent on *patient not home* visits
    B. *decrease* in the doctor's time in the clinics
    C. *increase* in the time spent by volunteers in the clinics
    D. *decrease* in the time spent by nurses in the office

18. Assume that you were newly assigned to replace a supervisor who had created resent-   18.____
ment among the staff by her authoritarian methods.
In order to secure acceptance by the staff, it would be BEST for you to

    A. concentrate on the managerial aspects of supervision until the staff has learned to
accept you
    B. continue authoritarian supervision for a while, tapering it off gradually as the staff
becomes accustomed to democratic methods
    C. explain democratic supervision at an early staff meeting and let the staff know that
they will now have more freedom
    D. maintain authoritarian methods but appeal to the staff for their loyal cooperation

19. A council of social agencies is a community agency which   19.____

    A. acts as a social planning agency for those organizations in the community that
belong to the council
    B. registers identifying information about families known to social agencies
    C. supplies confidential information about families known to social agencies
    D. acts as a money raising group for social agencies

20. Of the following statements, the one which BEST represents one of the values of vital   20.____
statistics in public health is: A(n)

    A. study of birth registration data shows the causes of infant deaths
    B. study of national mortality statistics will point out ways to save the lives of mothers
and newborn babies
    C. analysis of morbidity statistics will indicate the prevalence of certain diseases that
constitute health problems
    D. analysis of mortality statistics will help to estimate the possibility of epidemics

21. Administration of school health services is a difficult problem because of the official   21.____
responsibilities of both public health agencies and departments of education for the welfare of the school age child. There are arguments in favor of administration for each group.
However, of the following, the MOST valid argument in favor of administration by official public health agencies is that

    A. educators are not qualified by either experience or education to understand the
health problems of children
    B. the supervision of school nurses and physicians can best be done by a public
health agency
    C. departments of health are by law responsible for the protection of health and the
prevention of disease

D. educators are primarily interested in their own specific educational problems and exhibit only secondary interest in the health program

22. In order to make the best use of available public health nursing personnel in school health services, it is essential that nurses in the schools carry out only those functions which require their skills and judgment.
Of the following functions, the one which could BEST be delegated to *non-nursing* personnel is

    A. caring for acute injuries and illnesses
    B. instructing teachers and assisting them with the health observation of children
    C. assisting physicians with medical examinations
    D. reviewing physicians' recommendations and planning for follow-up

22.____

23. In making field observations, it is usually MOST advisable for the supervisor

    A. not to let the nurse know when she will be observed
    B. to select with the staff nurse the cases to be observed
    C. to observe the nurse on the day when the nurse invites her to do so
    D. to allow the nurse to select the cases she wishes the supervisor to observe

23.____

24. The recommended ratio of supervisors to staff nurses in public health nursing is one supervisor to _____ students.

    A. twelve staff workers, including
    B. ten staff nurses, including
    C. six graduate staff nurses and two
    D. eight workers, including

24.____

25. The National Institute of Mental Health of the Public Health Service has as its MAJOR purpose

    A. financial aid to states to provide better care for the indigent mentally ill
    B. stimulation of research in medical schools into the causes of mental illness
    C. training of mental health personnel, and assistance in developing community mental health programs
    D. case finding and treatment of people with mild mental disorders, to prevent the development of more severe psychoses

25.____

―――――――

KEY (CORRECT ANSWERS)

1.	C	11.	B
2.	C	12.	A
3.	A	13.	D
4.	D	14.	D
5.	B	15.	C
6.	D	16.	D
7.	A	17.	A
8.	D	18.	A
9.	B	19.	A
10.	D	20.	C

21.	C
22.	C
23.	B
24.	B
25.	C

EXAMINATION SECTION
TEST 1

DIRECTIONS: Each question or incomplete statement is followed by several suggested answers or completions. Select the one that BEST answers the question or completes the statement. *PRINT THE LETTER OF THE CORRECT ANSWER IN THE SPACE AT THE RIGHT.*

1. The aim of organization of a health department is to arrange people into working groups, associating those with similar functions or purposes in order to   1.____

   A. more efficiently obtain a desired result from group action
   B. provide proper channels for supervision
   C. assure staff development
   D. give the administrator a clear and concise picture of his staff

2. The goal of supervision in a nursing service is to   2.____

   A. see that the policies of the nursing service are carried out
   B. help nursing and ancillary personnel improve their skills and knowledge
   C. encourage the cooperation of nursing personnel so that the workload is evenly distributed
   D. improve nursing service to the community

3. Of the 21 critical objectives in the Healthy People 2010 initiative, which of the following is directly related to chronic disease prevention among adolescents and young adults?   3.____

   A. Reduce the proportion of children and adolescents who are overweight or obese
   B. Increase the proportion of adolescents who participate in daily school physical education
   C. Increase the proportion of school-based health centers with an oral health component
   D. Increase the proportion of schools that have a nurse-to-student ratio of at least 1:750

4. *Administratively,* the supervisor's PRINCIPAL function in a nursing service is to   4.____

   A. keep reliable schedules of nursing assignments and cases
   B. facilitate and further the service programs of the department
   C. screen problems for referral to administration
   D. consult with the health officer on administrative procedures

5. What piece of legislation requires Medicare-participating hospitals to establish and publicly report unit-by-unit staffing plans?   5.____

   A. Patient Protection and Affordable Care Act
   B. Registered Nurse Safe Staffing Act
   C. Medicare Modernization Act
   D. Social Security Act

6. The home visit is one of the most frequently used and highly regarded methods of pro- 6.____
viding service to the family.
The CHIEF advantage of the home visit over other methods is that it

   A. is less expensive and less time consuming than some group methods
   B. provides a better opportunity for the nurse to seek out new health problems
   C. permits the nurse to relate in a more meaningful way the experiences of other fam-
   ilies with similar problems which might be helpful in this situation
   D. permits the nurse to see the home and family in action for a more accurate
   appraisal of family relationships

7. When planning to visit a patient in her home for the first time, the nurse should be aware 7.____
that the PRIMARY purpose of a *first* visit is to

   A. gain information and build rapport
   B. analyze the health needs of the family
   C. teach the patient about her illness
   D. give information regarding available health facilities in the community

8. The supervised home visit as a method of professional guidance in nursing *ideally* MUST 8.____

   A. include a planning conference and an evaluation conference immediately after the
   visit
   B. provide for the supervisor's participation in nursing care during the visit
   C. allow opportunity for the supervisor to instruct the nurse during the visit
   D. be planned for a time when all members of the family are present

9. Of the following, the MOST advisable way for a supervising nurse to arrange for field vis- 9.____
its is to

   A. go when the nurse invites her to visit
   B. announce her visit without prior warning to the nurse
   C. plan the time and cases she will see with her staff
   D. plan her visits on a 6-month basis and post the schedule

10. The one of the following which is MOST essential in patient teaching by the nurse is the 10.____

   A. availability of health education literature in the health center
   B. provision for privacy during teaching conferences between supervisor and nurse
   C. maintenance of frequent contacts with the same patient
   D. nurse's ability to recognize teaching opportunities

11. Miss A., a nurse, told her supervisor that she felt that her visit to Mrs. Brown, who had 11.____
just returned home following a hysterectomy, was unproductive because she was unable
to teach Mrs. Brown the things she had planned for this visit. The supervisor asked the
nurse to briefly review her visit and, during the discussion, attempted to develop recognition of some positive accomplishments.
In this situation, the supervisor is practicing the principle of supervision which encour-
ages the nurse to

   A. practice critical analysis of an assignment
   B. make a self-evaluation of each planned visit
   C. gain some degree of security in the job
   D. make very definite plans for any home visit

12. The field visit is a valuable supervisory procedure, keeping the supervisor in close touch with the realities of the work to be done.
In utilizing this procedure, the supervisor SHOULD

    A. be certain that the staff nurse fully accepts this method of supervision
    B. participate actively in the field visit as a method of reinforcing the cooperative relationship between supervisor and nurse
    C. concentrate upon observing every minute detail of the service which the nurse is rendering
    D. precede the visit by careful preparation to help the nurse accept and utilize this form of supervision

12.____

13. There is one school of thought in nursing supervision which believes that the supervised home visit is not an appropriate supervisory method.
The MAIN reason underlying this conviction is that

    A. graduate nurses have been certified as competent by the schools which graduated them
    B. the supervisor cannot know all the patient's problems in one visit
    C. the nurse-patient relationship is distorted by the introduction of a stranger
    D. there are more economic methods of supervision available

13.____

14. A planned orientation program is essential for the introduction of the new staff nurse to the job.
In order for this orientation to be as efficient and economical as possible, it should have for its *primary* goal the

    A. adjustment of the nurse to her new job and environment
    B. rapid absorption of the nurse into the service
    C. training of the nurse in the techniques essential for job performance
    D. elimination of certain inhibiting factors which the new nurse brings with her to the job

14.____

15. The training period for newly-appointed nurses should

    A. include the same content for all newly employed staff
    B. vary according to previous experience
    C. be planned so that it can be completed within the period of probation
    D. be developed around individual supervisory conferences

15.____

16. The assignment of cases during the preliminary period is an important aspect of the induction of a new worker.
Of the following, the statement which provides the BEST guide for the assignment of cases to a new nurse is that

    A. every attempt should be made to provide the experience of handling every possible type of case during this period
    B. her case load should be kept very light during this period in order to allow the new worker to become adjusted to the work
    C. cases should be selected with the idea of providing this nurse with an opportunity to try out her relationships with families and to see the function of the nurse in providing continuity of care
    D. cases should be selected that will hold her interest and provide a challenge to her

16.____

17. Continuing staff education activities as a responsibility of a nursing service are *necessary* CHIEFLY because

    A. only about one-third of the nurses have adequate training
    B. quality of service is closely related to staff development
    C. shared staff experiences help in the development of the individual nurse
    D. present-day case loads are too heavy to allow the nurse to plan her own continued education

17.____

18. The *objectives* of the on-going education program in a nursing service should be established

    A. on the basis of the previous experience records of staff
    B. in conference, by the director and supervisors
    C. cooperatively by all of the staff
    D. by the public health nurse section of the local professional nursing organization

18.____

19. The one of the following which is NOT characteristic of workshop activities is that the

    A. direction of the discussion and the activities are planned and carried out by the group
    B. experiences and knowledge of the group itself are used in defining and solving problems
    C. procedures are organized around problems presented by the participants
    D. procedures are organized around the formal presentation of a body of subject matter

19.____

20. The PRIMARY purpose of keeping records in nursing is to

    A. provide a basis for studying the service given by the agency in terms of meeting community health needs
    B. provide better health care to patients and families in the community
    C. furnish information for collection of epidemiological data
    D. assist in the evaluation of a nurse's performance in the field

20.____

21. Process recording has been recommended as a supervisory method for the introduction of new staff nurses and field students.
One DISADVANTAGE of the method is that the

    A. supervisor is unable to observe the complete situation including, particularly, the skills, tone of voice, and mannerisms of the nurse
    B. effectiveness of the record is minimized because it is a verbatim account rather than a summary of the visit
    C. procedure is too time-consuming to produce effective advantages for improving performance in interviewing and in enriching the teaching content of visits
    D. motivation for continuous self-evaluation by the nurse is lessened

21.____

22. Of the following, the one that represents the BEST basis for planning the content of a successful staff development program is the

    A. time available for meetings
    B. chief health problems of the community

22.____

C. common needs of the nurses as related to the situations with which they are dealing
D. experimental programs conducted by other agencies

23. Assume that a newly assigned supervising nurse calls her first staff conference with the nurses under her supervision.
Of the following, the BEST approach to the group in this *initial* conference is for the supervisor

    23.____

    A. after greeting the group, to explain that she will be making some changes in the method of supervision and in the schedules and to express her confidence that each nurse will cooperate with her as changes occur
    B. to learn from the group common practices and procedures and ways of relating to the previous supervisor and to assure them that only as the supervisor and nurses get to know each other better will any changes or essential adjustments be made if necessary
    C. to make use of this initial meeting for a brief, friendly introduction on a social rather than a business level and to postpone any questions or comments from the group until a subsequent meeting
    D. to encourage each nurse to talk freely about herself and any problems around her work in order to ascertain similarities or differences among the group members as a focus for supervision

24. Assume that you have arranged an individual conference with one of your staff nurses to discuss problems she has encountered in one of her cases.
The one of the following on which it is MOST desirable for the supervisor to focus is the

    24.____

    A. handling of the case in terms of departmental procedures
    B. nurse in terms of her educational background
    C. potential resources
    D. patient's problems in terms of his needs

25. The individual conference between nurse and supervisor has great potential for staff guidance and teaching. In planning for an individual conference with a nurse, the FUNDAMENTAL concept that should guide all conference procedures is that

    25.____

    A. the conference should provide an opportunity for staff and supervisor to discuss problems important to both and together to develop greater capacity to meet future problems
    B. the supervisor should keep control of the individual conference at all times in order to insure adequate time for covering the fundamental problems of the nurse
    C. the supervisor should subordinate all of her own thinking to that of the staff nurse so that the nurse can develop proper insight and initiative for future occasions
    D. it is important to allow sufficient time for the conference in order to permit establishing of cooperative relationships

———

KEY (CORRECT ANSWERS)

1.	A		11.	C
2.	D		12.	D
3.	A		13.	C
4.	B		14.	A
5.	B		15.	B
6.	D		16.	C
7.	A		17.	B
8.	A		18.	C
9.	C		19.	D
10.	D		20.	B

21.	A
22.	C
23.	B
24.	D
25.	A

———

TEST 2

DIRECTIONS: Each question or incomplete statement is followed by several suggested answers or completions. Select the one that BEST answers the question or completes the statement. *PRINT THE LETTER OF THE CORRECT ANSWER IN THE SPACE AT THE RIGHT.*

1. Suppose that one of your experienced nurses who has been carrying an assignment that requires great skill is leaving.
   Of the following, the LEAST appropriate way to select a replacement for this assignment is to

   A. ask the more skilled members of your staff individually if they are interested in this assignment
   B. review the educational backgrounds of present staff members
   C. consider the work performance of the present staff
   D. ask the staff group in conference for a volunteer for this assignment

   1.____

2. A graduate student assigned to work with you asks to be excused for two days for personal reasons and states she will make up the time before the end of her assignment. As the supervisor, it would be MOST advisable for you to

   A. grant this request as it seems reasonable
   B. advise the student to ask her faculty instructor to speak to you about this request
   C. refuse this request since it will interfere with the schedule of work
   D. question the student to see if her request is justified

   2.____

3. Assume that you have noticed that one of the nurses under your supervision avoids making antepartal visits whenever possible. During field observation of this nurse on an antepartal visit, you found it to be quite superficial, and in your conference with her, she admits that she feels inadequate on such visits.
   Of the following, the LEAST helpful action for you to take in this situation is to

   A. assign several more antepartal cases for her to visit without supervision
   B. suggest that she take a course on the subject at one of the local universities
   C. give her some selected readings on the subject
   D. plan to observe her more frequently on such cases

   3.____

4. A new nurse recently assigned to your office asks you whether it is better to write records in the patient's home or in the office.
   Of the following, the LEAST desirable statement for you to make to the nurse in your discussion with her is that

   A. all records, to be accurate, must be written in the patient's home
   B. case material which requires some organization and thought may better be written away from the home
   C. the nurse should rely upon her own judgment as to which place is better adapted to the recording of the type of information she must have for her records
   D. recording of certain information in the home, such as temperature or symptoms of illness, would seem to be necessary

   4.____

5. Suppose that a written directive has been received initiating a new policy on visits to adults in need of rehabilitation nursing.
   The FIRST thing that the supervisor should do in this situation is to

   A. issue a memorandum to the staff describing the new policy
   B. arrange for a staff conference to discuss the new policy
   C. plan a detailed education program to teach the staff how to make such visits
   D. arrange for observation by her staff of rehabilitation nursing in another agency

   5.____

6. A nurse formerly in your office who resigned recently to return to school calls you to request that she be allowed to review some records to get material for a term paper.
   Of the following, the BEST action for you to take, since you are not sure of the department's policy on this type of request, is to

   A. plan an appropriate time for her to come in for this review since she is a former staff member known to your office
   B. explain that this is not possible because all records are confidential
   C. secure as much information as possible from her and explain that you will call her back after discussing her request with administration
   D. question her about the details of the paper and, if it seems worthwhile, grant her request

   6.____

7. One of the nurses under your supervision tells you she is having some difficulty with her husband.
   Of the following, the MOST appropriate action for you to take is to

   A. listen sympathetically but make no comments
   B. suggest possible ways for the nurse to solve her problem
   C. explore the problem with the nurse to see if she can resolve it for herself
   D. discourage her from discussing the problem with you but suggest sources of help

   7.____

8. You find that an increasing number of your staff are not following a certain procedure as directed in the manual.
   Of the following, the BEST course of action for you to take is to

   A. plan a group conference to explain that you want them to follow the set procedure at all times
   B. arrange a group conference and discuss this with your staff in order to learn why procedure is not being followed
   C. discuss this with each nurse who is not following procedure and explain that she must follow the instructions in the manual
   D. issue a written directive advising all nurses to consult their manuals on this matter

   8.____

9. Routine checking of records by the supervisor is *advisable* CHIEFLY in order to

   A. maintain standards of service
   B. keep the supervisor and, through her, the director informed of services rendered to the community
   C. evaluate the performance of individual nurses on an objective basis
   D. reduce the cost of service to the community

   9.____

10. When evaluating personnel, it is ESSENTIAL that individual differences be understood and accepted by both the individual employee and the supervisor so that the evaluation

    10.____

A. does not result in a feeling of frustration for the employee
B. makes the individual who is being rated aware that she has shortcomings
C. can be used as a yardstick for appraising the work of the entire staff
D. results in acceptance by the employee of all of the supervisor's suggestions

11. Assume that during your observation of a nurse in the field she asks you for an evalua-   11.____
tion of her work, which you feel was not as good as you had expecte
Of the following, the BEST action for you to take is to

A. discuss the visit with her immediately, frankly and in detail
B. avoid any discussion of the situation or visit by guiding conversation away from the subject
C. tell her that her work indicated both strengths and weaknesses but that you would like to discuss the details later in the office
D. tell her you would rather not discuss the visit with her until after you have reviewed the case record in the office

12. Present-day managerial practices advocate that adequate biographical levels of commu-   12.____
nication be maintained among all levels of nursing management.
Of the following, the BEST way to accomplish this is with

A. interdepartmental memoranda *only*
B. intradepartmental memoranda *only*
C. periodic staff meetings, interdepartmental and intradepartmental memoranda
D. interdepartmental and intradepartmental memoranda

13. It is generally agreed upon that it is important to have effective communications in the   13.____
nursing unit so that everyone knows exactly what is expected of him.
Of the following, the communications system which can assist in fulfilling this objective
BEST is one which consists of

A. written policies and procedures for administrative functions and verbal policies and procedures for professional functions
B. written policies and procedures for professional and administrative functions
C. verbal policies and procedures for professional and administrative functions
D. verbal policies and procedures for professional functions

14. If a head nurse wishes to build an effective department, she, *most generally*, must   14.____

A. be able to hire and fire as she feels necessary
B. consider the total aspects of her job, her influence and the effects of her decisions
C. have access to reasonable amounts of personnel and money with which to build her programs
D. attend as many professional conferences as possible so that she can keep up to date with all the latest advances in the field

15. Of the following, the factor which generally contributes MOST effectively to the perfor-   15.____
mance of the nursing unit is that the senior nurse

A. personally inspect the work of all employees
B. service clients at a faster rate than her subordinates
C. have an exact knowledge of formulary
D. implement a program of professional development for her staff

16. Nursing workload reports compare workload to   16.____

    A.   available professional time   B.   number of patients served
    C.   nurses' time devoted to it   D.   nursing personnel budget

17. Administrative policies relate MOST closely to   17.____

    A.   control of commodities and personnel
    B.   general policies emanating from the nursing office
    C.   fiscal management of the department *only*
    D.   handling and dispensing of drugs

18. Part of being a good supervisor is to be able to develop an attitude towards employees   18.____
which will motivate them to do their best on the jo
The *good* nurse-supervisor, therefore, should

    A.   take an interest in subordinates, but not develop an all-consuming attitude in this
        area
    B.   remain in an aloof position when dealing with employees
    C.   be as close to subordinates as possible on the job
    D.   take a complete interest in all the activities of subordinates, both on and off the job

19. The practice of a supervisor assigning an experienced nurse to train new nurses instead   19.____
of training them herself is generally considered

    A.   *undesirable;* the more experienced nurse will resent being taken away from her
        regular job
    B.   *desirable;* the supervisor can then devote more time to her regular duties
    C.   *undesirable;* the more experienced nurse is not working at the proper level to train
        new employees
    D.   *desirable;* the more experienced nurse is probably a better trainer than the supervi-
        sor

20. It is generally agreed that on-the-job training is MOST effective when new nurses are   20.____

    A.   provided with study manuals, standard operating procedures, and other written
        materials to be studied for at least two weeks before the nurses attempt to do the
        job
    B.   shown how to do the job in detail, and then instructed to do the work under close
        supervision
    C.   trained by an experienced nurse for at least a week to make certain that the new
        nurses can do the job
    D.   given work immediately which is checked at the end of each day

21. Nurses sometimes form small informal groups, commonly called cliques.   21.____
With regard to the effect of such groups on processing of the workload, the attitude a
supervisor should take towards these cliques is that of

    A.   *acceptance,* since they take the nurses' minds off their work without wasting too
        much time
    B.   *rejection,* since those nurses inside the clique tend to do less work than the outsid-
        ers
    C.   *acceptance,* since the supervisor is usually included in the clique
    D.   *rejection,* since they are usually disliked by higher management

22. Of the following, the BEST statement regarding rules and regulations in a nursing unit is that they

    22.____

    A. are *necessary evils* to be tolerated by those at and above the first supervisory level only
    B. are stated in broad, indefinite terms so as to allow maximum amount of leeway in complying with them
    C. must be understood by all nurses in the unit
    D. are primarily for management's needs since insurance regulations mandate them

23. It is sometimes considered desirable for a nursing supervisor to survey the opinions of her nurses before taking action on decisions affecting them.
Of the following, the greatest DISADVANTAGE of following this approach is that the nurses might

    23.____

    A. use this opportunity to complain rather than to make constructive suggestions
    B. lose respect for their supervisor whom they feel cannot make her own decisions
    C. regard this as an attempt by the supervisor to get ideas for which she can later claim credit
    D. be resentful if their suggestions are not adopted

24. Of the following, the MOST important reason for keeping statements of duties of nursing employees up to date is to

    24.____

    A. serve as a basis of information for other governmental jurisdictions
    B. enable the department of personnel to develop job-related examinations
    C. differentiate between levels within the nursing occupational group
    D. enable each nursing employee to know what her duties are

25. Of the following, the BEST way to evaluate the progress of a new subordinate is to

    25.____

    A. compare the output of the new nurse from week to week as to quantity and quality
    B. obtain the opinions of the new nurse's co-workers
    C. test the new nurse periodically to see how much she has learned
    D. hold frequent discussions with the nurse, focusing on her work

—————

KEY (CORRECT ANSWERS)

1.	D		11.	C
2.	B		12.	C
3.	A		13.	B
4.	A		14.	B
5.	B		15.	D
6.	C		16.	A
7.	D		17.	A
8.	B		18.	A
9.	A		19.	B
10.	A		20.	B

21.	A
22.	C
23.	D
24.	D
25.	A

———

EXAMINATION SECTION
TEST 1

DIRECTIONS: Each question or incomplete statement is followed by several suggested answers or completions. Select the one that BEST answers the question or completes the statement. *PRINT THE LETTER OF THE CORRECT ANSWER IN THE SPACE AT THE RIGHT.*

1. Of the following, the BEST definition of supervision in nursing is that it is   1._____

    A. the direction and critical evaluation of instruction
    B. overseeing the work of the staff nurse for direction and correction
    C. inspection of all services with authority to make needed changes
    D. expert technical service designed to improve conditions of work in nursing
    E. a cooperative educational process designed to improve the service rendered

2. The PRIMARY purpose of supervision in nursing is to   2._____

    A. promote the professional development of each staff nurse
    B. improve nursing service to the public
    C. get the work of the agency done with economy and efficiency
    D. induct new nurses into the service
    E. make the community aware of its health needs

3. A supervisor has difficulty with a staff nurse who is careless in her work and cannot be   3._____
depended on to carry out the work assigned to her. The supervisor believes this difficulty
is due to a resentment of supervision on the part of the staff nurse.
The BEST action for the supervisor to take in this situation is to

    A. recommend transfer to another office where the nurse can make a new start
    B. cultivate a personal friendship with the nurse to overcome her attitude toward supervision
    C. make frequent supervisory visits with the nurse to make her feel you are interested in her work
    D. give her an opportunity to act as your assistant so she will develop an appreciation of supervision
    E. find some phase of the work which she likes and does well, and give her recognition for her achievements

4. An unfavorable evaluation of a nurse's performance, substantiated by concrete facts, has   4._____
been discussed with the nurse. A written report is filed in the local office. Shortly after this,
the nurse is transferred to another office.
The BEST thing to do with the report in your office is to

    A. send it to the office to which the nurse has been transferred
    B. summarize the main points in a written report and send it to the central office
    C. destroy it
    D. give it to the nurse
    E. give a verbal report to the supervisor in the office to which the nurse has been transferred

5. Of the following statements, the one which represents the *minimum* amount of post-grad-   5._____
uate study recommended for nursing supervisors is:

A. No advanced study if supervisor has had one year of public health nursing experience under qualified supervision
B. The completion of 1 semester of advanced study
C. Completion of 1 year advanced study
D. Completion of a program of study approved by a national organization for nursing
E. The completion of an *approved* program of study, to include a course in the principles of supervision

6. Assume that you are newly appointed to a supervisory nursing position. The FIRST step you should take on assuming this new position is to

   6.____

A. make a survey to discover the health needs of the community
B. make friends with the staff to insure their cooperation
C. analyze the supervisory job to find out what you are responsible for
D. visit other community health and welfare agencies to become familiar with all phases of the agency program
E. make a field visit with each staff nurse to become familiar with all phases of the agency program

7. Successful supervision depends to a considerable extent on planning a program. Of the following factors, the one which is NOT relevant to the planning of such a program is:

   7.____

A. Finding out what needs to be done
B. Selecting the methods to be used
C. Scheduling the necessary activities
D. Allowing no obstacles to interfere with your plan
E. Evaluating the plan

8. The word *creative* applied to supervision in nursing means:

   8.____

A. Using scientific methods
B. Developing and applying new values and methods
C. Developing latent supervisory talent in staff nurses
D. Securing above average performance from each staff nurse
E. Developing new techniques for nursing procedures

9. Supervision in nursing is dependent for success on the qualifications of the supervisor herself. Of the following factors below, the one which will place the GREATEST limit on the *beginning* activities of a newly appointed supervisor is

   9.____

A. lack of advanced education in nursing
B. lack of information about the staff and the community
C. limited experience in nursing
D. lack of experience in public speaking
E. extreme shyness and lack of confidence in her abilities

10. For the purpose of improving nursing service to the community, the one of the following supervisory activities which should take *precedence* in emphasis and time is

   10.____

A. office administration
B. individual and group staff education
C. supervision of records

D. scheduling of work
E. field visits with nurses

11. Assume that a new policy has been adopted by the central office of your agency. A memorandum outlining this policy has been sent to each supervisor. You, as a supervisor, are not in accord with the administration on this new policy.
Of the following, the BEST procedure for you to follow in interpreting this policy to the staff nurses is to

    A. tell the staff it must be done since the order comes from the administrative head of the service
    B. report it to the staff without further explanation
    C. report it to the staff, but at the same time convey your reaction to the central office
    D. present the plan to the staff, ask them to try it out for a period and report results to you so that you can send a report to the central office
    E. suggest to the staff that they take action concerning the adoption of the policy at their staff council

11.____

12. The administrator of a nursing agency expects assistance from the supervisor in carrying out certain administrative functions.
Of the following administrative duties, the one which is NOT a function of the supervisor is:

    A. Assisting with planning new policies and evaluating old ones
    B. Administering the details of the service in accordance with established policies
    C. Assisting with the management of fiscal matters, such as budgeting and fundraising
    D. Coordinating and using effectively the services of other departments and branches of the service
    E. Promoting desirable personnel relationships through the development of a contented and efficient staff

12.____

13. The administrator expects the supervisor to promote staff development so that each nurse is functioning at her highest level of efficiency.
Of the following statements, the one which is the BEST criterion for judging the supervisor's effectiveness in achieving the optimum efficiency of each staff nurse is

    A. office management which allows the work to proceed with smoothness and efficiency
    B. organized procedures for the direct individual supervision of the staff nurses
    C. satisfactory working relationships among the staff
    D. the development of a sound staff education program
    E. organization of the work of each nurse so that she serves the families and agency to the best of her ability

13.____

14. The supervisor is expected to maintain good personnel relationships and personal job satisfaction for each staff member.
In an agency where staff salaries are inadequate, the course of action that would do the MOST to promote job satisfaction and morale is

    A. curtailing the agency problem and reducing the work load of the staff
    B. permitting the staff nurses to increase their income through additional work outside the agency, on holidays and weekends

14.____

   C. emphasizing the fact that the social obligation of the nurse to the community should take precedence over salary considerations

   D. interpreting administrative problems and efforts to the staff by having administrative officers discuss their problems and plans for action to the staff group

   E. encouraging the staff group to take action through their staff council to promote better salaries

15. Although the ultimate responsibility for the quality of nursing service rests with the staff nurse, the supervisor is responsible to the agency for all services rendered by the staff nurse.
Of the following, the supervisor can BEST discharge her responsibility in this respect by

   A. keeping rigid regulations at a minimum, and establishing guides based on the accepted principles of nursing

   B. scheduling each nurse's daily work to be sure she carries out all her assigned duties

   C. establishing standard methods and procedures to be used by all nurses in each service rendered

   D. having each nurse come in to the office, both morning and evening, to review with the supervisor her daily work report

   E. planning with each nurse a course of action to be followed for each family under her care

16. To aid her to develop her professional effectiveness as a nurse, the staff nurse expects guidance and assistance from the supervisor.
Of the following, the supervisor may carry out this function BEST by

   A. giving the nurse assignments only in the areas where she does her poorest work, since the best growth comes from overcoming weaknesses

   B. assisting each nurse to analyze her own work, find her strengths and weaknesses, but emphasizing her strengths and building on them

   C. ignoring the nurse's weaknesses, since through building on strengths, weaknesses will automatically be overcome

   D. assigning the nurse only to work she likes to do, since the best growth comes from satisfaction in the job

   E. keeping constantly before each nurse a concept of the *ideal* nurse, so she will not get in a rut through satisfaction with her performance

17. The staff nurse has a right to expect the supervisor to delegate authority and turn over to the staff some responsibility for independent action at the earliest possible moment.
Of the following responsibilities, the one for which the supervisor can allow *independent* action on the part of the staff at the earliest possible moment is

   A. planning and executing staff education programs

   B. developing new techniques for procedures

   C. determining new policies for administering the service

   D. planning and executing their own work assignments

   E. developing cooperative procedures for working with other community agencies

18. The MOST valid reason for preferring a *generalized* rather than a *specialized* nursing service in a community is that

A. a variety of work is stimulating to the staff nurses
B. it avoids friction among workers of various agencies
C. it provides better service at less cost to the community
D. it is easier to secure financial support because fewer demands are made on the public for funds
E. nurses today have better preparation for nursing and are equipped to carry out all phases of nursing service

19. Group instruction of patients by nurses is a modern trend in nursing service. The PRIMARY reason for emphasizing this type of service is that

19.____

A. nurses today are prepared to do group teaching
B. group teaching publicizes the service through reaching a larger number of people
C. it is less expensive for the agency
D. it makes more efficient use of available nursing service
E. it allows for an exchange of views among people with a variety of racial and educational backgrounds

20. A nurse should keep careful records of all families served. The CHIEF reason for this is that these records

20.____

A. show the social causes of illness
B. help to give better family health service
C. show how well the agency is meeting community needs
D. justify the agency budget
E. provide material for statistical reports

21. Of the following statements, the one which is the BEST guide for the selection of a case load for a new staff nurse during her period of introduction to a nursing agency is to involve her in

21.____

A. every possible type of case in order to give her a complete picture of the type of services given by the agency
B. cases presenting few health problems so she will not be discouraged by having difficult situations to face
C. cases where the health and social problems are varied and difficult since it is important during this period to discover the nurse's ability to solve family problems
D. cases which present the type of health problems which will give the new nurse an opportunity to see the function of the nurse in a family health program
E. cases involving contacts with many health and welfare agencies to give her a good picture of community health work

22. Of the following, the one which is the BEST criterion of the supervisor's ability is the ability to

22.____

A. mold the staff nurses into a desirable pattern established by the supervisor
B. organize the resources of the staff nurses with the maximum degree of efficiency
C. secure the consent of the staff nurses to follow established nursing policies
D. develop and maintain good working relationships with the administrative staff
E. secure the consent of the entire staff to the objectives which the supervisor has set up for her nursing program

23. One of the aims of supervision is to help the staff nurse achieve independence in plan-   23.____
ning and executing her work. Of the following methods, the one which would be MOST
likely to succeed with a new staff nurse who makes no attempt to plan her work and is,
therefore, unable to carry out her assignments is to

    A. reduce her case load to one she can manage with ease
    B. plan her work for her for a short period, so she will learn from you how to plan
    C. assign her as assistant to an older staff nurse who will plan her work for her
    D. give her daily guidance in planning her work, and increase her responsibility gradu-
       ally
    E. give her only one type of assignment at a time, and when she can plan that well,
       allow her to go on to another type

24. The CHIEF value of the field visit as an educational method of supervision in nursing is   24.____
that it

    A. gives the supervisor an opportunity to become familiar with the problems of fami-
       lies served by the agency
    B. stimulates self-evaluation on the part of the staff nurse
    C. gives the staff nurse an opportunity to demonstrate her ability in nursing tech-
       niques
    D. gives the supervisor an opportunity to test the effectiveness of her staff education
       program
    E. gives the supervisor an opportunity to secure information about the work of the
       staff nurse as an aid to guiding her in the solution of problems revealed

25. The individual conference between staff nurse and supervisor is an effective method of   25.____
supervision.
Of the following important factors, the one which is an *absolute essential,* without
which the presence of the other four factors would not guarantee success, is

    A. a good relationship between the nurse and the supervisor
    B. privacy during the conference
    C. sufficient time to allow both the nurse and the supervisor to discuss adequately the
       points each one wishes to make
    D. advance planning by both nurse and supervisor
    E. a written guide for the supervisor

_____

KEY (CORRECT ANSWERS)

1. E	11. D
2. B	12. C
3. E	13. E
4. B	14. D
5. E	15. A
6. C	16. B
7. D	17. D
8. B	18. C
9. C	19. D
10. B	20. B

21. D
22. B
23. D
24. E
25. A

———

READING COMPREHENSION
UNDERSTANDING AND INTERPRETING WRITTEN MATERIAL
EXAMINATION SECTION
TEST 1

Questions 1-8.

DIRECTIONS: Each question or incomplete statement is followed by several suggested answers or completions. Select the one that BEST answers the question or completes the statement. *PRINT THE LETTER OF THE CORRECT ANSWER IN THE SPACE AT THE RIGHT.*

Questions 1 and 2.

DIRECTIONS: Your answers to Questions 1 and 2 must be based ONLY on the information given in the following paragraph.

Hospitals maintained wholly by public taxation may treat only those compensation cases which are emergencies and may not treat such emergency cases longer than the emergency exists; provided, however, that these restrictions shall not be applicable where there is not available a hospital other than a hospital maintained wholly by taxation.

1. According to the above paragraph, compensation cases

    A. are regarded as emergency cases by hospitals maintained wholly by public taxation
    B. are seldom treated by hospitals maintained wholly by public taxation
    C. are treated mainly by privately endowed hospitals
    D. may be treated by hospitals maintained wholly by public taxation if they are emergencies

1.____

2. According to the above paragraph, it is MOST reasonable to conclude that where a privately endowed hospital is available,

    A. a hospital supported wholly by public taxation may treat emergency compensation cases only so long as the emergency exists
    B. a hospital supported wholly by public taxation may treat any compensation cases
    C. a hospital supported wholly by public taxation must refer emergency compensation cases to such a hospital
    D. the restrictions regarding the treatment of compensation cases by a tax-supported hospital are not wholly applicable

2.____

Questions 3-7.

DIRECTIONS: Answer Questions 3 through 7 ONLY according to the information given in the following passage.

THE MANUFACTURE OF LAUNDRY SOAP

The manufacture of soap is not a complicated process. Soap is a fat or an oil, plus an alkali, water and salt. The alkali used in making commercial laundry soap is caustic soda. The salt used is the same as common table salt. A fat is generally an animal product that is not a liquid at room temperature. If heated, it becomes a liquid. An oil is generally liquid at room temperature. If the temperature is lowered, the oil becomes a solid just like ordinary fat.

At the soap plant, a huge tank five stories high, called a *kettle*, is first filled part way with fats and then the alkali and water are added. These ingredients are then heated and boiled together. Salt is then poured into the top of the boiling solution; and as the salt slowly sinks down through the mixture, it takes with it the glycerine which comes from the melted fats. The product which finally comes from the kettle is a clear soap which has a moisture content of about 34%. This clear soap is then chilled so that more moisture is driven out. As a result, the manufacturer finally ends up with a commercial laundry soap consisting of 88% clear soap and only 12% moisture.

3.   An ingredient used in making laundry soap is   3.____

   A.   table sugar   B.   potash
   C.   glycerine   D.   caustic soda

4.   According to the above passage, a difference between fats and oils is that fats   4.____

   A.   cost more than oils
   B.   are solid at room temperature
   C.   have less water than oils
   D.   are a liquid animal product

5.   According to the above passage, the MAIN reason for using salt in the manufacture of   5.____
soap is to

   A.   make the ingredients boil together
   B.   keep the fats in the kettle melted
   C.   remove the glycerine
   D.   prevent the loss of water from the soap

6.   According to the passage, the purpose of chilling the clear soap is to   6.____

   A.   stop the glycerine from melting
   B.   separate the alkali from the fats
   C.   make the oil become solid
   D.   get rid of more moisture

7.   According to the passage, the percentage of moisture in commercial laundry soap is   7.____

   A.   12%   B.   34%   C.   66%   D.   88%

8. The x-ray has gone into business. Developed primarily to aid in diagnosing human ills, the machine now works in packing plants, in foundries, in service stations, and in a dozen ways to contribute to precision and accuracy in industry.
The above statement means *most nearly* that the x-ray

    8.____

    A.   was first developed to aid business
    B.   is of more help to business than it is to medicine
    C.   is being used to improve the functioning of business
    D.   is more accurate for packing plants than it is for foundries

Questions 9-25.

DIRECTIONS: Each question consists of a statement. You are to indicate whether the statement is TRUE (T) or FALSE (F). *PRINT THE LETTER OF THE CORRECT ANSWER IN THE SPACE AT THE RIGHT.*

Questions 9-12.

DIRECTIONS: Read the paragraph below about *shock* and then answer Questions 9 through 12 according to the information given in the paragraph.

<u>SHOCK</u>

While not found in all injuries, shock is present in all serious injuries caused by accidents. During shock, the normal activities of the body slow down. This partly explains why one of the signs of shock is a pale, cold skin, since insufficient blood goes to the body parts during shock.

9.   If the injury caused by an accident is serious, shock is sure to be present.

    9.____

10.   In shock, the heart beats faster than normal.

    10.____

11.   The face of a person suffering from shock is usually red and flushed.

    11.____

12.   Not enough blood goes to different parts of the body during shock.

    12.____

Questions 13-18.

DIRECTIONS: Questions 13 through 18, inclusive, are to be answered SOLELY on the basis of the information contained in the following statement and NOT upon any other information you may have.

Blood transfusions are given to patients at the hospital upon recommendation of the physicians attending such cases. The physician fills out a *Request for Blood Transfusion* form in duplicate and sends both copies to the Medical Director's office, where a list is maintained of persons called *donors* who desire to sell their blood for transfusions. A suitable donor is selected, and the transfusion is given. Donors are, in many instances, medical students and employees of the hospital. Donors receive twenty-five dollars for each transfusion.

13.   According to the above paragraph, a blood donor is paid twenty-five dollars for each transfusion.

    13.____

14. According to the above paragraph, only medical students and employees of the hospital are selected as blood donors.   14._____

15. According to the above paragraph, the *Request for Blood Transfusion* form is filled out by the patient and sent to the Medical Director's office.   15._____

16. According to the above paragraph, a list of blood donors is maintained in the Medical Director's office.   16._____

17. According to the above paragraph, cases for which the attending physicians recommend blood transfusions are usually emergency cases.   17._____

18. According to the above paragraph, one copy of the *Request for Blood Transfusion* form is kept by the patient and one copy is sent to the Medical Director's office.   18._____

Questions 19-25.

DIRECTIONS: Questions 19 through 25, inclusive, are to be answered SOLELY on the basis of the information contained in the following passage and NOT upon any other information you may have.

Before being admitted to a hospital ward, a patient is first interviewed by the Admitting Clerk, who records the patient's name, age, sex, race, birthplace, and mother's maiden name. This clerk takes all of the money and valuables that the patient has on his person. A list of the valuables is written on the back of the envelope in which the valuables are afterwards placed. Cash is counted and placed in a separate envelope, and the amount of money and the name of the patient are written on the outside of the envelope. Both envelopes are sealed, fastened together, and placed in a compartment of a safe.

An orderly then escorts the patient to a dressing room where the patient's clothes are removed and placed in a bundle. A tag bearing the patient's name is fastened to the bundle. A list of the contents of the bundle is written on property slips, which are made out in triplicate. The information contained on the outside of the envelopes containing the cash and valuables belonging to the patient is also copied on the property slips.

According to the above passage,

19. patients are escorted to the dressing room by the Admitting Clerk.   19._____

20. the patient's cash and valuables are placed together in one envelope.   20._____

21. the number of identical property slips that are made out when a patient is being admitted to a hospital ward is three.   21._____

22. the full names of both parents of a patient are recorded by the Admitting Clerk before a patient is admitted to a hospital ward.   22._____

23. the amount of money that a patient has on his person when admitted to the hospital is entered on the patient's property slips.   23._____

24. an orderly takes all the money and valuables that a patient has on his person.   24._____

25. the patient's name is placed on the tag that is attached to the bundle containing the patient's clothing.   25._____

KEY (CORRECT ANSWERS)

1.	D		11.	F
2.	A		12.	T
3.	D		13.	T
4.	B		14.	F
5.	C		15.	F
6.	D		16.	T
7.	A		17.	T
8.	C		18.	F
9.	T		19.	F
10.	F		20.	F

21.	T
22.	F
23.	T
24.	F
25.	T

TEST 2

DIRECTIONS: Each question or incomplete statement is followed by several suggested answers or completions. Select the one that BEST answers the question or completes the statement. *PRINT THE LETTER OF THE CORRECT ANSWER IN THE SPACE AT THE RIGHT.*

Questions 1-4.

DIRECTIONS: Questions 1 through 4 are to be answered in accordance with the following paragraphs.

One fundamental difference between the United States health care system and the health care systems of some European countries is the way that hospital charges for long-term illnesses affect their citizens.

In European countries such as England, Sweden, and Germany, citizens can face, without fear, hospital charges due to prolonged illness, no matter how substantial they may be. Citizens of these nations are required to pay nothing when they are hospitalized, for they have prepaid their treatment as taxpayers when they were well and were earning incomes.

On the other hand, the United States citizen, in spite of the growth of payments by third parties which include private insurance carriers as well as public resources, has still to shoulder 40 percent of hospital care costs, while his private insurance contributes only 25 percent and public resources the remaining 35 percent.

Despite expansion of private health insurance and social legislation in the United States, out-of-pocket payments for hospital care by individuals have steadily increased. Such payments, currently totalling $23 billion, are nearly twice as high as ten years ago.

Reform is inevitable and, when it comes, will have to reconcile sharply conflicting interests. Hospital staffs are demanding higher and higher wages. Hospitals are under pressure by citizens, who as patients demand more and better services but who as taxpayers or as subscribers to hospital insurance plans, are reluctant to pay the higher cost of improved care. An acceptable reconciliation of these interests has so far eluded legislators and health administrators in the United States.

1. According to the above passage, the one of the following which is an ADVANTAGE that citizens of England, Sweden, and Germany have over United States citizens is that, when faced with long-term illness,

    1.____

    A. the amount of out-of-pocket payments made by these European citizens is small when compared to out-of-pocket payments made by United States citizens
    B. European citizens have no fear of hospital costs no matter how great they may be
    C. more efficient and reliable hospitals are available to the European citizen than is available to the United States citizens
    D. a greater range of specialized hospital care is available to the European citizens than is available to the United States citizens

2. According to the above passage, reform of the United States system of health care must reconcile all of the following EXCEPT   2.____

    A. attempts by health administrators to provide improved hospital care
    B. taxpayers' reluctance to pay for the cost of more and better hospital services
    C. demands by hospital personnel for higher wages
    D. insurance subscribers' reluctance to pay the higher costs of improved hospital care

3. According to the above passage, the out-of-pocket payments for hospital care that individuals made ten years ago was APPROXIMATELY _____ billion.   3.____

    A. $32   B. $23   C. $12   D. $3

4. According to the above passage, the GREATEST share of the costs of hospital care in the United States is paid by   4.____

    A. United States citizens   B. private insurance carriers
    C. public resources   D. third parties

Questions 5-8.

DIRECTIONS: Questions 5 through 8 are to be answered SOLELY on the basis of the information contained in the following passage.

Effective cost controls have been difficult to establish in most hospitals in the United States. Ways must be found to operate hospitals with reasonable efficiency without sacrificing quality and in a manner that will reduce the amount of personal income now being spent on health care and the enormous drain on national resources. We must adopt a new public objective of providing higher quality health care at significantly lower cost. One step that can be taken to achieve this goal is to carefully control capital expenditures for hospital construction and expansion. Perhaps the way to start is to declare a moratorium on all hospital construction and to determine the factors that should be considered in deciding whether a hospital should be built. Such factors might include population growth, distance to the nearest hospital, availability of medical personnel, and hospital bed shortage.

A second step to achieve the new objective is to increase the ratio of out-of-hospital patient to in-hospital patient care. This can be done by using separate health care facilities other than hospitals to attract patients who have increasingly been going to hospital clinics and overcrowding them. Patients should instead identify with a separate health care facility to keep them out of hospitals.

A third step is to require better hospital operating rules and controls. This step might include the review of a doctor's performance by other doctors, outside professional evaluations of medical practice, and required refresher courses and re-examinations for doctors. Other measures might include obtaining mandatory second opinions on the need for surgery in order to avoid unnecessary surgery, and outside review of work rules and procedures to eliminate unnecessary testing of patients.

A fourth step is to halt the construction and public subsidizing of new medical schools and to fill whatever needs exist in professional coverage by emphasizing the medical training of physicians with specialities that are in short supply and by providing a better geographic distribution of physicians and surgeons.

5. According to the above passage, providing higher quality health care at lower cost can
be achieved by the

    A. greater use of out-of-hospital facilities
    B. application of more effective cost controls on doctors' fees
    C. expansion of improved in-hospital patient care services at hospital clinics
    D. development of more effective training programs in hospital administration

5.____

6. According to the above passage, the one of the following which should be taken into
account in determining if a hospital should be constructed is the

    A. number of out-of-hospital health care facilities
    B. availability of public funds to subsidize construction
    C. number of hospitals under construction
    D. availability of medical personnel

6.____

7. According to the above passage, it is IMPORTANT to operate hospitals efficiently
because

    A. they are currently in serious financial difficulties
    B. of the need to reduce the amount of personal income going to health care
    C. the quality of health care services has deteriorated
    D. of the need to increase productivity goals to take care of the growing population in
the United States

7.____

8. According to the above passage, which one of the following approaches is MOST
LIKELY to result in better operating rules and controls in hospitals?

    A. Allocating doctors to health care facilities on the basis of patient population
    B. Equalizing the workloads of doctors
    C. Establishing a physician review board to evaluate the performance of other physi-
cians
    D. Eliminating unnecessary outside review of patient testing

8.____

Questions 9-14.

DIRECTIONS: Questions 9 through 14 are to be answered SOLELY on the basis of the information contained in the following passage.

    The United States today is the only major industrial nation in the world without a system
of national health insurance or a national health service. Instead, we have placed our prime
reliance on private enterprise and private health insurance to meet the need. Yet, in a recent
year, of the 180 million Americans under 65 years of age, 34 million had no hospital insurance, 38 million had no surgical insurance, 63 million had no out-patient x-ray and laboratory
insurance, 94 million had no insurance for prescription drugs, and 103 million had no insurance for physician office visits or home visits. Some 35 million Americans under the age of 65
had no health insurance whatsoever. Some 64 million additional Americans under age 65 had
health insurance coverage that was less than that provided to the aged under Medicare.

Despite more than three decades of enormous growth, the private health insurance industry today pays benefits equal to only one-third of the total cost of private health care, leaving the rest to be borne by the patient—essentially the same ratio which held true a decade ago. Moreover, nearly all private health insurance is limited; it provides partial benefits, not comprehensive benefits; acute care, not preventive care; it siphons off the young and healthy, and ignores the poor and medically indigent. The typical private carrier usually pays only the cost of hospital care, forcing physicians and patients alike to resort to wasteful and inefficient use of hospital facilities, thereby giving further impetus to the already soaring costs of hospital care. Valuable hospital beds are used for routine tests and examinations. Unnecessary hospitalization, unnecessary surgery, and unnecessarily extended hospital stays are encouraged. These problems are exacerbated by the fact that administrative costs of commercial carriers are substantially higher than they are for Blue Shield, Blue Cross, or Medicare.

9. According to the above passage, the PROPORTION of total private health care costs paid by private health insurance companies today as compared to ten years ago has   9._____

   A. *increased* by approximately one-third
   B. *remained* practically the same
   C. *increased* by approximately two-thirds
   D. *decreased* by approximately one-third

10. According to the above passage, the one of the following which has contributed MOST to wasteful use of hospital facilities is the   10._____

   A. increased emphasis on preventive health care
   B. practice of private carriers of providing comprehensive health care benefits
   C. increased hospitalization of the elderly and the poor
   D. practice of a number of private carriers of paying only for hospital care costs

11. Based on the information in the above passage, which one of the following patients would be LEAST likely to receive benefits from a typical private health insurance plan?   11._____
   A

   A. young patient who must undergo an emergency appendectomy
   B. middle-aged patient who needs a costly series of x-ray and laboratory tests for diagnosis of gastrointestinal complaints
   C. young patient who must visit his physician weekly for treatment of a chronic skin disease
   D. middle-aged patient who requires extensive cancer surgery

12. Which one of the following is the MOST accurate inference that can be drawn from the above passage?   12._____

   A. Private health insurance has failed to fully meet the health care needs of Americans.
   B. Most Americans under age 65 have health insurance coverage better than that provided to the elderly under Medicare.
   C. Countries with a national health service are likely to provide poorer health care for their citizens than do countries that rely primarily on private health insurance.
   D. Hospital facilities in the United States are inadequate to meet the nation's health care needs.

13. Of the total number of Americans under age 65, what percentage belonged in the combined category of persons with NO health insurance or health insurance less than that provided to the aged under Medicare?

    A. 19%   B. 36%   C. 55%   D. 65%

13.____

14. According to the above passage, the one of the following types of health insurance which covered the SMALLEST number of Americans under age 65 was

    A. hospital insurance
    B. surgical insurance
    C. insurance for prescription drugs
    D. insurance for physician office or home visits

14.____

Questions 15-17.

DIRECTIONS: Questions 15 through 17 are to be answered SOLELY on the basis of the information contained in the following passage.

Statistical studies have demonstrated that disease and mortality rates are higher among the poor than among the more affluent members of our society. Periodic surveys conducted by the United States Public Health Service continue to document a higher prevalence of infectious and chronic diseases within low income families. While the basic life style and living conditions of the poor are to a considerable extent responsible for this less favorable health status, there are indications that the kind of health care received by the poor also plays a significant role. The poor are less likely to be aware of the concepts and practices of scientific medicine and less likely to seek health care when they need it. Moreover, they are discouraged from seeking adequate health care by the depersonalization, disorganization, and inadequate emphasis on preventive care which characterize the health care most often provided for them.

To achieve the objective of better health care for the poor, the following approaches have been suggested: encouraging the poor to seek preventive care as well as care for acute illness and to establish a lasting one-to-one relationship with a single physician who can treat the poor patient as a whole individual; sufficient financial subsidy to put the poor on an equal footing with *paying patients,* thereby giving them the opportunity to choose from among available health services providers; inducements to health services providers to establish public clinics in poverty areas; and legislation to provide for health education, earlier detection of disease, and coordinated health care.

15. According to the above passage, the one of the following which is a function of the United States Public Health Service is

    A. gathering data on the incidence of infectious diseases
    B. operating public health clinics in poverty areas lacking private physicians
    C. recommending legislation for the improvement of health care in the United States
    D. encouraging the poor to participate in programs aimed at the prevention of illness

15.___

16. According to the above passage, the one of the following which is MOST characteristic of the health care currently provided for the poor is that it   16.____

     A. aims at establishing clinics in poverty areas
     B. enables the poor to select the health care they want through the use of financial subsidies
     C. places insufficient stress on preventive health care
     D. over-emphasizes the establishment of a one-to-one relationship between physician and patient

17. The above passage IMPLIES that the poor lack the financial resources to   17.____

     A. obtain adequate health insurance coverage
     B. select from among existing health services
     C. participate in health education programs
     D. lobby for legislation aimed at improving their health care

Questions 18-20.

DIRECTIONS: Questions 18 through 20 are to be answered SOLELY on the basis of the information contained in the following passage.

The concept of *affiliation,* developed more than ten years ago, grew out of a series of studies which found evidence of faulty care, surgery of *questionable* value and other undesirable conditions in the city's municipal hospitals. The affiliation agreements signed shortly thereafter were designed to correct these deficiencies by assuring high quality medical care. In general, the agreements provided the staff and expertise of a voluntary hospital—sometimes connected with a medical school—to operate various services or, in some cases, all of the professional divisions of a specific municipal hospital. The municipal hospitals have paid for these services, which last year cost the city $200 million, the largest single expenditure of the Health and Hospitals Corporation. In addition, the municipal hospitals have provided to the voluntary hospitals such facilities as free space for laboratories and research. While some experts agree that affiliation has resulted in improvements in some hospital care, they contend that many conditions that affiliation was meant to correct still exist. In addition, accountability procedures between the Corporation and voluntary hospitals are said to be so inadequate that audits of affiliation contracts of the past five years revealed that there may be more than $200 million in charges for services by the voluntary hospitals which have not been fully substantiated. Consequently, the Corporation has proposed that future agreements provide accountability in terms of funds, services supplied, and use of facilities by the voluntary hospitals.

18. According to the above passage, *affiliation* may BEST be defined as an agreement whereby   18.____

     A. voluntary hospitals pay for the use of municipal hospital facilities
     B. voluntary and municipal hospitals work to eliminate duplication of services
     C. municipal hospitals pay voluntary hospitals for services performed
     D. voluntary and municipal hospitals transfer patients to take advantage of specialized services

19. According to the above passage, the MAIN purpose for setting up the *affiliation* agreement was to

19.____

    A. supplement the revenues of municipal hospitals
    B. improve the quality of medical care in municipal hospitals
    C. reduce operating costs in municipal hospitals
    D. increase the amount of space available to municipal hospitals

20. According to the above passage, inadequate accountability procedures have resulted in

20.____

    A. unsubstantiated charges for services by the voluntary hospitals
    B. emphasis on research rather than on patient care in municipal hospitals
    C. unsubstantiated charges for services by the municipal hospitals
    D. economic losses to voluntary hospitals

Questions 21-25.

DIRECTIONS: Questions 21 through 25 are to be answered SOLELY on the basis of the information contained in the following passage.

The payment for medical services covered under the Outpatient Medical Insurance Plan (OMI) may be made, by OMI, directly to a physician or to the OMI patient. If the physician and the patient agree that the physician is to receive payment directly from OMI, the payment will be officially assigned to the physician; this is the assignment method. If payment is not assigned, the patient receives payment directly from OMI based on an itemized bill he submits, regardless of whether or not he has already paid his physician.

When a physician accepts assignment of the payment for medical services, he agrees that total charges will not be more than the allowed charge determined by the OMI carrier administering the program. In such cases, the OMI patient pays any unmet part of the $85 annual deductible, plus 10 percent of the remaining charges to the physician. In unassigned claims, the patient is responsible for the total amount charged by the physician. The patient will then be reimbursed by the program 90 percent of the allowed charges in excess of the annual deductible.

The rates of acceptance of assignments provide a measure of how many OMI patients are spared *administrative participation* in the program. Because physicians are free to accept or reject assignments, the rate in which assignments are made provide a general indication of the medical community's satisfaction with the OMI program, especially with the level of amounts paid by the program for specific services and the promptness of payment.

21. According to the above passage, in order for a physician to receive payment directly from OMI for medical services to an OMI patient, the physician would have to accept the assignment of payment, to have the consent of the patient, AND to

21.____

    A. submit to OMI a paid itemized bill
    B. collect from the patient 90% of the total bill
    C. collect from the patient the total amount of the charges for his services, a portion of which he will later reimburse the patient
    D. agree that his charges for services to the patient will not exceed the amount allowed by the program

22. According to the above passage, if a physician accepts assignment of payment, the patient pays

    22.____

    A. the total amount charged by the physician and is reimbursed by the program for 90 percent of the allowed charges in excess of the applicable deductible
    B. any unmet part of the $85 annual deductible, plus 90 percent of the remaining charges
    C. the total amount charged by the physician and is reimbursed by the program for 10 percent of the allowed charges in excess of the $85 annual deductible
    D. any unmet part of the $85 annual deductible, plus 10 percent of the remaining charges

23. A physician has accepted the assignment of payment for charges to an OMI patient. The physician's charges, all of which are allowed under OMI, amount to $115. This is the first time the patient has been eligible for OMI benefits and the first time the patient has received services from this physician.
According to the above passage, the patient must pay the physician

    23.____

    A. $27   B. $76.50   C. $88   D. $103.50

24. In an unassigned claim, a physician's charges, all of which are allowed under OMI, amount to $165. The patient paid the physician the full amount of the bill.
If this is the FIRST time the patient has been eligible for OMI benefits, he will receive from OMI a reimbursement of

    24.____

    A. $72   B. $80   C. $85   D. $93

25. According to the above passage, if the rate of acceptance of assignments by physicians is high, it is LEAST appropriate to conclude that the medical community is generally satisfied with the

    25.____

    A. supplementary medical insurance program
    B. levels of amounts paid to physicians by the program
    C. number of OMI patients being spared administrative participation in the program
    D. promptness of the program in making payment for services

---

KEY (CORRECT ANSWERS)

1.	B	11.	C	21.	D
2.	A	12.	A	22.	D
3.	C	13.	C	23.	C
4.	D	14.	D	24.	A
5.	A	15.	A	25.	C
6.	D	16.	C		
7.	B	17.	B		
8.	C	18.	C		
9.	B	19.	B		
10.	D	20.	A		

PREPARING WRITTEN MATERIAL

EXAMINATION SECTION
TEST 1

DIRECTIONS : Each of the sentences in the tests that follow may be classified under one of the following four categories:

    A. *Incorrect* because of faulty grammar or sentence structure
    B. *Incorrect* because of faulty punctuation
    C. *Incorrect* because of faulty capitalization
    D. *Correct*

Examine each sentence carefully to determine under which of the above four options it is best classified. Then, in the space on the right, print the capital letter preceding the option which is the *BEST* of the four suggested above.

(Each incorrect sentence contains but one type of error. Consider a sentence to be correct if it contains none of the types of errors mentioned, even though there may be other correct ways of expressing the same thought.)

1. This fact, together with those brought out at the previous meeting, prove that the schedule is satisfactory to the employees.   1.____

2. Like many employees in scientific fields, the work of bookkeepers and accountants requires accuracy and neatness.   2.____

3. "What can I do for you," the secretary asked as she motioned to the visitor to take a seat.   3.____

4. Our representative, Mr. Charles will call on you next week to determine whether or not your claim has merit.   4.____

5. We expect you to return in the spring; please do not disappoint us.   5.____

6. Any supervisor, who disregards the just complaints of his subordinates, is remiss in the performance of his duty.   6.____

7. Because she took less than an hour for lunch is no reason for permitting her to leave before five o'clock.   7.____

8. "Miss Smith," said the supervisor, "Please arrange a meeting of the staff for two o'clock on Monday."   8.____

9. A private company's vacation and sick leave allowance usually differs considerably from a public agency.   9.____

10. Therefore, in order to increase the efficiency of operations in the department, a report on the recommended changes in procedures was presented to the departmental committee in charge of the program.   10.____

11. We told him to assign the work to whoever was available.   11.____

12. Since John was the most efficient of any other employee in the bureau, he received the highest service rating.   12.____

13. Only those members of the national organization who resided in the middle West   13._____
    attended the conference in Chicago.

14. The question of whether the office manager has as yet attained, or indeed can ever hope   14._____
    to secure professional status is one which has been discussed for years.

15. No one knew who to blame for the error which, we later discovered, resulted in a consid-   15._____
    erable loss of time.

KEY (CORRECT ANSWERS)

1.	A	6.	B
2.	A	7.	A
3.	B	8.	C
4.	B	9.	A
5.	D	10.	D

11.	D
12.	A
13.	C
14.	B
15.	A

TEST 2

DIRECTIONS : Each of the sentences in the tests that follow may be classified under one of
the following four categories:

      A. *Incorrect* because of faulty grammar or sentence structure
      B. *Incorrect* because of faulty punctuation
      C. *Incorrect* because of faulty capitalization
      D. *Correct*

1. The National alliance of Businessmen is trying to persuade private businesses to hire   1.____
youth in the summertime.

2. The supervisor who is on vacation, is in charge of processing vouchers.   2.____

3. The activity of the committee at its conferences is always stimulating.   3.____

4. After checking the addresses again, the letters went to the mailroom.   4.____

5. The director, as well as the employees, are interested in sharing the dividends.   5.____

KEY (CORRECT ANSWERS)

1. C
2. B
3. D
4. A
5. A

TEST 3

DIRECTIONS: In each of the following groups of sentences, one of the four sentences is faulty in grammar, punctuation, or capitalization. Select the incorrect sentence in each case.

1.   A.   Sailing down the bay was a thrilling experience for me.   1._____
     B.   He was not consulted about your joining the club.
     C.   This story is different than the one I told you yesterday.
     D.   There is no doubt about his being the best player.

2.   A.   He maintains there is but one road to world peace.   2._____
     B.   It is common knowledge that a child sees much he is not supposed to see.
     C.   Much of the bitterness might have been avoided if arbitration had been resorted to earlier in the meeting.
     D.   The man decided it would be advisable to marry a girl somewhat younger than him.

3.   A.   In this book, the incident I liked least is where the hero tries to put out the forest   3._____
          fire.
     B.   Learning a foreign language will undoubtedly give a person a better understanding of his mother tongue.
     C.   His actions made us wonder what he planned to do next.
     D.   Because of the war, we were unable to travel during the summer vacation.

4.   A.   The class had no sooner become interested in the lesson than the dismissal bell   4._____
          rang.
     B.   There is little agreement about the kind of world to be planned at the peace conference.
     C.   "Today," said the teacher, "we shall read 'The Wind in the Willows.' I am sure you'll like it.
     D.   The terms of the legal settlement of the family quarrel handicapped both sides for many years.

5.   A.   I was so suprised that I was not able to say a word.   5._____
     B.   She is taller than any other member of the class.
     C.   It would be much more preferable if you were never seen in his company.
     D.   We had no choice but to excuse her for being late.

KEY (CORRECT ANSWERS)

1. C
2. D
3. A
4. C
5. C

TEST 4

DIRECTIONS: In each of the following groups of sentences, one of the four sentences is faulty in grammar, punctuation, or capitalization. Select the incorrect sentence in each case.

1. A. Please send me these data at the earliest opportunity.
   B. The loss of their material proved to be a severe handicap.
   C. My principal objection to this plan is that it is impracticable.
   D. The doll had laid in the rain for an hour and was ruined.

   1.____

2. A. The garden scissors, left out all night in the rain, were in a badly rusted condition.
   B. The girls felt bad about the misunderstanding which had arisen.
   C. Sitting near the campfire, the old man told John and I about many exciting adventures he had had.
   D. Neither of us is in a position to undertake a task of that magnitude.

   2.____

3. A. The general concluded that one of the three roads would lead to the besieged city.
   B. The children didn't, as a rule, do hardly anything beyond what they were told to do.
   C. The reason the girl gave for her negligence was that she had acted on the spur of the moment.
   D. The daffodils and tulips look beautiful in that blue vase.

   3.____

4. A. If I was ten years older, I should be interested in this work.
   B. Give the prize to whoever has drawn the best picture.
   C. When you have finished reading the book, take it back to the library.
   D. My drawing is as good as or better than yours.

   4.____

5. A. He asked me whether the substance was animal or vegetable.
   B. An apple which is unripe should not be eaten by a child.
   C. That was an insult to me who am your friend.
   D. Some spy must of reported the matter to the enemy.

   5.____

6. A. Limited time makes quoting the entire message impossible.
   B. Who did she say was going?
   C. The girls in your class have dressed more dolls this year than we.
   D. There was such a large amount of books on the floor that I couldn't find a place for my rocking chair.

   6.____

7. A. What with his sleeplessness and his ill health, he was unable to assume any responsibility for the success of the meeting.
   B. If I had been born in February, I should be celebrating my birthday soon.
   C. In order to prevent breakage, she placed a sheet of paper between each of the plates when she packed them.
   D. After the spring shower, the violets smelled very sweet.

   7.____

8. A. He had laid the book down very reluctantly before the end of the lesson.
   B. The dog, I am sorry to say, had lain on the bed all night.
   C. The cloth was first lain on a flat surface; then it was pressed with a hot iron.
   D. While we were in Florida, we lay in the sun until we were noticeably tanned.

   8.____

9.   A.   If John was in New York during the recent holiday season, I have no doubt he spent   9.____
             most of his time with his parents.
      B.   How could he enjoy the television program; the dog was barking and the baby
             was crying.
      C.   When the problem was explained to the class, he must have been asleep.
      D.   She wished that her new dress were finished so that she could go to the party.

10.   A.   The engine not only furnishes power but light and heat as well.   10.____
      B.   You're aware that we've forgotten whose guilt was established, aren't you?
      C.   Everybody knows that the woman made many sacrifices for her children.
      D.   A man with his dog and gun is a familiar sight in this neighborhood.

———

KEY (CORRECT ANSWERS)

1.	D	6.	D
2.	C	7.	B
3.	B	8.	C
4.	A	9.	B
5.	D	10.	A

———

TEST 5

DIRECTIONS: Each of Questions 1 to 15 consists of a sentence which may be classified appropriately under one of the following four categories:
   A. *Incorrect* because of faulty grammar
   B. *Incorrect* because of faulty punctuation
   C. *Incorrect* because of faulty spelling
   D. *Correct*

Examine each sentence carefully. Then, print, in the space on the right, the letter preceding the category which is the best of the four suggested above.

(Note: Each incorrect sentence contains only one type of error. Consider a sentence correct if it contains no errors, although there may be other correct ways of writing the sentence.)

1. Of the two employees, the one in our office is the most efficient. 1._____

2. No one can apply or even understand, the new rules and regulations. 2._____

3. A large amount of supplies were stored in the empty office. 3._____

4. If an employee is occassionally asked to work overtime, he should do so willingly. 4._____

5. It is true that the new procedures are difficult to use but, we are certain that you will learn them quickly. 5._____

6. The office manager said that he did not know who would be given a large allotment under the new plan. 6._____

7. It was at the supervisor's request that the clerk agreed to postpone his vacation. 7._____

8. We do not believe that it is necessary for both he and the clerk to attend the conference. 8._____

9. All employees, who display perseverance, will be given adequate recognition. 9._____

10. He regrets that some of us employees are dissatisfied with our new assignments. 10._____

11. "Do you think that the raise was merited," asked the supervisor? 11._____

12. The new manual of procedure is a valuable supplament to our rules and regulations. 12._____

13. The typist admitted that she had attempted to pursuade the other employees to assist her in her work. 13._____

14. The supervisor asked that all amendments to the regulations be handled by you and I. 14._____

15. The custodian seen the boy who broke the window. 15._____

KEY (CORRECT ANSWERS)

1.	A	6.	D
2.	B	7.	D
3.	A	8.	A
4.	C	9.	B
5.	B	10.	D

11.	B
12.	C
13.	C
14.	A
15.	A

PREPARING WRITTEN MATERIAL

PARAGRAPH REARRANGEMENT
COMMENTARY

The sentences which follow are in scrambled order. You are to rearrange them in proper order and indicate the letter choice containing the correct answer at the space at the right.

Each group of sentences in this section is actually a paragraph presented in scrambled order. Each sentence in the group has a place in that paragraph; no sentence is to be left out. You are to read each group of sentences and decide upon the best order in which to put the sentences so as to form as well-organized paragraph.

The questions in this section measure the ability to solve a problem when all the facts relevant to its solution are not given.

More specifically, certain positions of responsibility and authority require the employee to discover connections between events sometimes, apparently, unrelated. In order to do this, the employee will find it necessary to correctly infer that unspecified events have probably occurred or are likely to occur. This ability becomes especially important when action must be taken on incomplete information.

Accordingly, these questions require competitors to choose among several suggested alternatives, each of which presents a different sequential arrangement of the events. Competitors must choose the MOST logical of the suggested sequences.

In order to do so, they may be required to draw on general knowledge to infer missing concepts or events that are essential to sequencing the given events. Competitors should be careful to infer only what is essential to the sequence. The plausibility of the wrong alternatives will always require the inclusion of unlikely events or of additional chains of events which are NOT essential to sequencing the given events.

It's very important to remember that you are looking for the best of the four possible choices, and that the best choice of all may not even be one of the answers you're given to choose from.

There is no one right way to solve these problems. Many people have found it helpful to first write out the order of the sentences, as they would have arranged them, on their scrap paper before looking at the possible answers. If their optimum answer is there, this can save them some time. If it isn't, this method can still give insight into solving the problem. Others find it most helpful to just go through each of the possible choices, contrasting each as they go along. You should use whatever method feels comfortable, and works, for you.

While most of these types of questions are not that difficult, we've added a higher percentage of the difficult type, just to give you more practice. Usually there are only one or two questions on this section that contain such subtle distinctions that you're unable to answer confidently, and you then may find yourself stuck deciding between two possible choices, neither of which you're sure about.

Preparing Written Material

EXAMINATION SECTION
TEST 1

DIRECTIONS: The following groups of sentences need to be arranged in an order that makes sense. Select the letter preceding the sequence that represents the best sentence order. *PRINT THE LETTER OF THE CORRECT ANSWER IN THE SPACE AT THE RIGHT.*

Question 1

1.____

1. The ostrich egg shell's legendary toughness makes it an excellent substitute for certain types of dishes or dinnerware, and in parts of Africa ostrich shells are cut and decorated for use as containers for water.
2. Since prehistoric times, people have used the enormous egg of the ostrich as a part of their diet, a practice which has required much patience and hard work-to hard-boil an ostrich egg takes about four hours.
3. Opening the egg's shell, which is rock hard and nearly an inch thick, requires heavy tools, such as a saw or chisel; from inside, a baby ostrich must use a hornlike projection on its beak as a miniature pick-axe to escape from the egg.
4. The offspring of all higher-order animals originate from single egg cells that are carried by mothers, and most of these eggs are relatively small, often microscopic.
5. The egg of the African ostrich, however, weighs a massive thirty pounds, making it the largest single cell on earth, and a common object of human curiosity and wonder.

The best order is

A. 5 4 1 2 3
B. 1 4 5 3 2
C. 4 2 3 5 1
D. 4 5 2 3 1

Question 2

2.____

1. Typically only a few feet high on the open sea, individual tsunami have been known to circle the entire globe two or three times if their progress is not interrupted, but are not usually dangerous until they approach the shallow water that surrounds land masses.
2. Some of the most terrifying and damaging hazards caused by earthquakes are tsunami, which were once called "tidal waves"— a poorly chosen name, since these waves have nothing to do with tides.
3. Then a wave, slowed by the sudden drag on the lower part of its moving water column, will pile upon itself, sometimes reaching a height of over 100 feet.
4. Tsunami (Japanese for "great harbor wave") are seismic waves that are caused by earthquakes near oceanic trenches, and once triggered, can travel up to 600 miles an hour on the open ocean.
5. A land-shoaling tsunami is capable of extraordinary destruction; some tsunami have deposited large boats miles inland, washed out two-foot-thick seawalls, and scattered locomotive trains over long distances.

The best order is

A. 4 1 3 2 5
B. 1 3 4 2 5
C. 5 1 3 2 4
D. 2 4 1 3 5

Question 3   3._____

1. Soon, by the 1940's, jazz was the most popular type of music among American intellectuals and college students.
2. In the early days of jazz, it was considered "lowdown" music, or music that was played only in rough, disreputable bars and taverns.
3. However, jazz didn't take long to develop from early ragtime melodies into more complex, sophisticated forms, such as Charlie Parker's "bebop" style of jazz.
4. After charismatic band leaders such as Duke Ellington and Count Basic brought jazz to a larger audience, and jazz continued to evolve into more complicated forms, white audiences began to accept and even to enjoy the new American art form.
5. Many white Americans, who then dictated the tastes of society, were wary of music that was played almost exclusively in black clubs in the poorer sections of cities and towns.

The best order is

A. 5 4 3 2 1
B. 2 5 3 4 1
C. 4 5 3 1 2
D. 1 2 4 3 5

Question 4   4._____

1. Then, hanging in a windless place, the magnetized end of the needle would always point to the south.
2. The needle could then be balanced on the rim of a cup, or the edge of a fingernail, but this balancing act was hard to maintain, and the needle often fell off.
3. Other needles would point to the north, and it was important for any traveler finding his way with a compass to remember which kind of magnetized needle he was carrying.
4. To make some of the earliest compasses in recorded history, ancient Chinese "magicians" would rub a needle with a piece of magnetized iron called a lodestone.
5. A more effective method of keeping the needle free to swing with its magnetic pull was to attach a strand of silk to the center of the needle with a tiny piece of wax.

The best order is

A. 4 2 5 1 3
B. 4 3 5 2 1
C. 4 5 2 1 3
D. 4 1 3 5 2

Question 5

5.____

1. The now-famous first mate of the *HMS Bounty,* Fletcher Christian, founded one of the world's most peculiar civilizations in 1790.
2. The men knew they had just committed a crime for which they could be hanged, so they set sail for Pitcairn, a remote, abandoned island in the far eastern region of the Polynesian archipelago, accompanied by twelve Polynesian women and six men.
3. In a mutiny that has become legendary, Christian and the others forced Captain Bligh into a lifeboat and set him adrift off the coast of Tonga in April of 1789.
4. In early 1790, the *Bounty* landed at Pitcairn Island, where the men lived out the rest of their lives and founded an isolated community which to this day includes direct descendants of Christian and the other crewmen.
5. The *Bounty,* commanded by Captain William Bligh, was in the middle of a global voyage, and Christian and his shipmates had come to the conclusion that Bligh was a reckless madman who would lead them to their deaths unless they took the ship from him.

The best order is

A. 4 5 3 2 1
B. 1 3 5 2 4
C. 1 5 3 2 4
D. 3 1 5 4 2

Question 6

6.____

1. But once the vines had been led to make orchids, the flowers had to be carefully hand-pollinated, because unpollinated orchids usually lasted less than a day, wilting and dropping off the vine before it had even become dark.
2. The Totonac farmers discovered that looping a vine back around once it reached a five-foot height on its host tree would cause the vine to flower.
3. Though they knew how to process the fruit pods and extract vanilla's flavoring agent, the Totonacs also knew that a wild vanilla vine did not produce abundant flowers or fruit.
4. Wild vines climbed along the trunks and canopies of trees, and this constant upward growth diverted most of the vine's energy to making leaves instead of the orchid flowers that, once pollinated, would produce the flavorful pods.
5. Hundreds of years before vanilla became a prized food flavoring in Europe and the Western World, the Totonac Indians of the Mexican Gulf Coast were skilled cultivators of the vanilla vine, whose fruit they literally worshipped as a goddess.

The best order is

A. 2 3 4 1 5
B. 2 4 3 1 5
C. 5 3 4 2 1
D. 3 4 1 2 5

Question 7

7.____

1. Once airborne, the spider is at the mercy of the air currents—usually the spider takes a brief journey, traveling close to the ground, but some have been found in air samples collected as high as 10,000 feet, or been reported landing on ships far out at sea.
2. Once a young spider has hatched, it must leave the environment into which it was born as quickly as possible, in order to avoid competing with its hundreds of brothers and sisters for food.
3. The silk rises into warm air currents, and as soon as the pull feels adequate the spider lets go and drifts up into the air, suspended from the silk strand in the same way that a person might parasail.
4. To help young spiders do this, many species have adapted a practice known as "aerial dispersal," or, in common speech, "ballooning."
5. A spider that wants to leave its surroundings quickly will climb to the top of a grass stem or twig, face into the wind, and aim its back end into the air, releasing a long stream of silk from the glands near the tip of its abdomen.

The best order is

    A. 5 4 2 3 1
    B. 5 2 4 1 3
    C. 2 5 4 3 1
    D. 2 4 5 3 1

Question 8

8.____

1. For about a year, Tycho worked at a castle in Prague with a scientist named Johannes Kepler, but their association was cut short by another argument that drove Kepler out of the castle, to later develop, on his own, the theory of planetary orbits.
2. Tycho found life without a nose embarrassing, so he made a new nose for himself out of silver, which reportedly remained glued to his face for the rest of his life.
3. Tycho Brahe, the 17th-century Danish astronomer, is today more famous for his odd and arrogant personality than for any contribution he has made to our knowledge of the stars and planets.
4. Early in his career, as a student at Rostock University, Tycho got into an argument with the another student about who was the better mathematician, and the two became so angry that the argument turned into a sword fight, during which Tycho's nose was sliced off.
5. Later in his life, Tycho's arrogance may have kept him from playing a part in one of the greatest astronomical discoveries in history: the elliptical orbits of the solar system's planets.

The best order is

    A. 1 4 2 3 5
    B. 4 2 3 5 1
    C. 4 2 1 3 5
    D. 3 4 2 5 1

Question 9

9.____

1. The processionaries are so used to this routine that if a person picks up the end of a silk line and brings it back to the origin—creating a closed circle—the caterpillars may travel around and around for days, sometimes starving ar freezing, without changing course.
2. Rather than relying on sight or sound, the other caterpillars, who are lined up end-to-end behind the leader, travel to and from their nests by walking on this silk line, and each will reinforce it by laying down its own marking line as it passes over.
3. In order to insure the safety of individuals, the processionary caterpillar nests in a tree with dozens of other caterpillars, and at night, when it is safest, they all leave together in search of food.
4. The processionary caterpillar of the European continent is a perfect illustration of how much some insect species rely on instinct in their daily routines.
5. As they leave their nests, the processionaries form a single-file line behind a leader who spins and lays out a silk line to mark the chosen path.

The best order is

A. 4 3 5 2 1
B. 3 5 4 2 1
C. 3 5 2 1 4
D. 4 5 3 1 2

Question 10

10.____

1. Often, the child is also given a handcrafted walker or push cart, to provide support for its first upright explorations.
2. In traditional Indian families, a child's first steps are celebrated as a ceremonial event, rooted in ancient myth.
3. These carts are often intricately designed to resemble the chariot of Krishna, an important figure in Indian mythology.
4. The sound of these anklet bells is intended to mimic the footsteps of the legendary child Rama, who is celebrated in devotional songs throughout India.
5. When the child's parents see that the child is ready to begin walking, they will fit it with specially designed ankle bracelets, adorned with gently ringing bells.

The best order is

A. 2 3 4 1 5
B. 2 5 3 1 4
C. 5 4 1 3 2
D. 5 3 2 1 4

Question 11   11._____

1. The settlers planted Osage orange all across Middle America, and today long lines and rectangles of Osage orange trees can still be seen on the prairies, running along the former boundaries of farms that no longer exist.

2. After trying sod walls and water-filled ditches with no success, American farmers began to look for a plant that was adaptable to prairie weather, and that could be trimmed into a hedge that was "pig-tight, horse-high, and bull-strong."

3. The tree, so named because it bore a large (but inedible) fruit the size of an orange, was among the sturdiest and hardiest of American trees, and was prized among Native Americans for the strength and flexibility of bows which were made from its wood.

4. The first people to practice agriculture on the American flatlands were faced with an important problem: what would they use to fence their land in a place that was almost entirely without trees or rocks?

5. Finally, an Illinois farmer brought the settlers a tree that was native to the land between the Red and Arkansas rivers, a tree called the Osage orange.

The best order is

    A. 2 1 5 3 4
    B. 1 2 3 4 5
    C. 4 2 5 3 1
    D. 4 2 1 3 5

Question 12   12._____

1. After about ten minutes of such spirited and complicated activity, the head dancer is free to make up his or her own movements while maintaining the interest of the New Year's crowd.

2. The dancer will then perform a series of leg kicks, while at the same time operating the lion's mouth with his own hand and moving the ears and eyes by means of a string which is attached to the dancer's own mouth.

3. The most difficult role of this dance belongs to the one who controls the lion's head; this person must lead all the other "parts" of the lion through the choreographed segments of the dance.

4. The head dancer begins with a complex series of steps, alternately stepping forward with the head raised, and then retreating a few steps while lowering the head, a movement that is intended to create the impression that the lion is keeping a watchful eye for anything evil.

5. When performing a traditional Chinese New Year's lion dance, several performers must fit themselves inside a large lion costume and work together to enact different parts of the dance.

The best order is

    A. 5 3 4 2 1
    B. 3 4 2 5 1
    C. 3 1 5 4 2
    D. 4 2 3 5 1

Question 13   13._____

1. For many years the shell of the chambered nautilus was treasured in Europe for its beauty and intricacy, but collectors were unaware that they were in possession of the structure that marked a "missing link" in the evolution of marine mollusks.
2. The nautilus, however, evolved a series of enclosed chambers in its shell, and invented a new use for the structure: the shell began to serve as a buoyancy device.
3. Equipped with this new flotation device, the nautilus did not need the single, muscular foot of its predecessors, but instead developed flaps, tentacles, and a gentle form of jet propulsion that transformed it into the first mollusk able to take command of its own destiny and explore a three-dimensional world.
4. By pumping and adjusting air pressure into the chambers, the nautilus could spend the day resting on the bottom, and then rise toward the surface at night in search of food.
5. The nautilus shell looks like a large snail shell, similar to those of its ancestors, who used their shells as protective coverings while they were anchored to the sea floor.

The best order is

    A. 5 2 4 1 3
    B. 5 1 2 3 4
    C. 1 2 5 3 4
    D. 1 5 2 4 3

Question 14   14._____

1. While France and England battled for control of the region, the Acadiens prospered on the fertile farmland, which was finally secured by England in 1713.
2. Early in the 17th century, settlers from western France founded a colony called Acadie in what is now the Canadian province of Nova Scotia.
3. At this time, English officials feared the presence of spies among the Acadiens who might be loyal to their French homeland, and the Acadiens were deported to spots along the Atlantic and Caribbean shores of America.
4. The French settlers remained on this land, under English rule, for around forty years, until the beginning of the French and Indian War, another conflict between France and England.
5. As the Acadien refugees drifted toward a final home in southern Louisiana, neighbors shortened their name to "Cadien," and finally "Cajun," the name which the descendants of early Acadiens still call themselves.

The best order is

    A. 1 4 2 3 5
    B. 2 1 3 5 4
    C. 2 1 4 3 5
    D. 5 2 3 4 1

Question 15   15.____

1. Traditional households in the Eastern and Western regions of Africa serve two meals a day-one at around noon, and the other in the evening.
2. The starch is then used in the way that Americans might use a spoon, to scoop up a portion of the main dish on the person's plate.
3. The reason for the starch's inclusion in every meal has to do with taste as well as nutrition; African food can be very spicy, and the starch is known to cool the burning effect of the main dish.
4. When serving these meals, the main dish is usually served on individual plates, and the starch is served on a communal plate, from which diners break off a piece of bread or scoop rice or fufu in their fingers.
5. The typical meals usually consist of a thick stew or soup as the main course, and an accompanying starch—either bread, rice, *or fufu, a* starchy grain paste similar in consistency to mashed potatoes.

The best order is

A. 5 2 3 4 1
B. 5 1 4 3 2
C. 1 4 5 3 2
D. 1 5 4 2 3

Question 16   16.____

1. In the early days of the American Midwest, Indiana settlers sometimes came together to hold an event called an apple peeling, where neighboring settlers gathered at the homestead of a host family to help prepare the hosts' apple crop for cooking, canning, and making apple butter.
2. At the beginning of the event, each peeler sat down in front of a ten- or twenty-gallon stone jar and was given a crock of apples and a paring knife.
3. Once a peeler had finished with a crock, another was placed next to him; if the peeler was an unmarried man, he kept a strict count of the number of apples he had peeled, because the winner was allowed to kiss the girl of his choice.
4. The peeling usually ended by 9:30 in the evening, when the neighbors gathered in the host family's parlor for a dance social.
5. The apples were peeled, cored, and quartered, and then placed into the jar.

The best order is

A. 1 5 3 4 2
B. 2 5 3 4 1
C. 1 2 5 3 4
D. 2 1 5 4 3

Question 17

17._____

1. If your pet turtle is a land turtle and is native to temperate climates, it will stop eating some time in October, which should be your cue to prepare the turtle for hibernation.
2. The box should then be covered with a wire screen, which will protect the turtle from any rodents or predators that might want to take advantage of a motionless and helpless animal.
3. When your turtle hasn't eaten for a while and appears ready to hibernate, it should be moved to its winter quarters, most likely a cellar or garage, where the temperature should range between 40° and 45° F.
4. Instead of feeding the turtle, you should bathe it every day in warm water, to encourage the turtle to empty its intestines in preparation for its long winter sleep.
5. Here the turtle should be placed in a well-ventilated box whose bottom is covered with a moisture-absorbing layer of clay beads, and then filled three-fourths full with almost dry peat moss or wood chips, into which the turtle will burrow and sleep for several months.

The best order is

A. 1 4 3 5 2
B. 3 4 2 5 1
C. 3 2 4 1 5
D. 4 5 2 3 1

Question 18

18._____

1. Once he has reached the nest, the hunter uses two sturdy bamboo poles like huge chopsticks to pull the nest away from the mountainside, into a large basket that will be lowered to people waiting below.
2. The world's largest honeybees colonize the Nepalese mountainsides, building honeycombs as large as a person on sheer rock faces that are often hundreds of feet high.
3. In the remote mountain country of Nepal, a small band of "honey hunters" carry out a tradition so ancient that 10,000 year-old drawings of the practice have been found in the caves of Nepal.
4. To harvest the honey and beeswax from these combs, a honey hunter climbs above the nests, lowers a long bamboo-fiber ladder over the cliff, and then climbs down.
5. Throughout this dangerous practice, the hunter is stung repeatedly, and only the veterans, with skin that has been toughened over the years, are able to return from a hunt without the painful swelling caused by stings.

The best order is

A. 2 4 3 5 1
B. 2 4 1 5 3
C. 5 3 2 4 1
D. 3 2 4 1 5

Question 19

19.____

1. After the Romans left Britain, there were relentless attacks on the islands from the barbarian tribes of northern Germany—the Angles, Saxons, and Jutes.
2. As the empire weakened, Roman soldiers withdrew from Britain, leaving behind a country that continued to practice the Christian religion that had been introduced by the Romans.
3. Early Latin writings tell of a Christian warrior named Arturius (Arthur, in English) who led the British citizens to defeat these barbarian invaders, and brought an extended period of peace to the lands of Britain.
4. Long ago, the British Isles were part of the far-flung Roman Empire that extended across most of Europe and into Africa and Asia.
5. The romantic legend of King Arthur and his knights of the Round Table, one of the most popular and widespread stories of all time, appears to have some foundation in history.

The best order is

A. 5 4 3 2 1
B. 5 4 2 1 3
C. 4 5 2 3 1
D. 4 3 2 1 5

Question 20

20.____

1. The cylinder was allowed to cool until it sould stand on its own, and then it was cut from the tube and split down the side with a single straight cut.
2. Nineteenth-century glassmakers, who had not yet discovered the glazier's modern techniques for making panes of glass, had to create a method for converting their blown glass into flat sheets.
3. The bubble was then pierced at the end to make a hole that opened up while the glassmaker gently spun it, creating a cylinder of glass.
4. Turned on its side and laid on a conveyor belt, the cylinder was strengthened, or tempered, by being heated again and cooled very slowly, eventually flattening out into a single rectangular piece of glass.
5. To do this, the glassmaker dipped the end of a long tube into melted glass and blew into the other end of the tube, creating an expanding bubble of glass.

The best order is

A. 2 5 3 4 1
B. 2 4 5 3 1
C. 3 5 2 4 1
D. 3 1 4 5 2

Question 21

21.____

1. The splints are almost always hidden, but horses are occasionally born whose splinted toes project from the leg on either side, just above the hoof.
2. The second and fourth toes remained, but shrank to thin splints of bone that fused invisibly to the horse's leg bone.
3. Horses are unique among mammals, having evolved feet that each end in what is essentially a single toe, capped by a large, sturdy hoof.
4. Julius Caesar, an emperor of ancient Rome, was said to have owned one of these three-toed horses, and considered it so special that he would not permit anyone else to ride it.
5. Though the horse's earlier ancestors possessed the traditional mammalian set of five toes on each foot, the horse has retained only its third toe; its first and fifth toes disappeared completely as the horse evolved.

The best order is

A. 3 5 2 1 4
B. 5 3 2 4 1
C. 3 2 5 1 4
D. 5 2 3 1 4

Question 22

22.____

1. The new building materials—some of which are twenty feet long, and weigh nearly six tons—were transported to Pohnpei on rafts, and were brought into their present position by using hibiscus fiber ropes and leverage to move the stone columns upward along the inclined trunks of coconut palm trees.
2. The ancestors built great fires to heat the stone, and then poured cool seawater on the columns, which caused the stone to contract and split along natural fracture lines.
3. The now-abandoned enclave of Nan Madol, a group of 92 man-made islands off the shore of the Micronesian island of Pohnpei, is estimated to have been built around the year 500 A.D.
4. The islanders say their ancestors quarried stone columns from a nearby island, where large basalt columns were formed by the cooling of molten lava.
5. The structures of Nan Madol are remarkable for the sheer size of some of the stone "logs" or columns that were used to create the walls of the offshore community, and today anthropologists can only rely on the information of existing local people for clues about how Nan Madol was built.

The best order is

A. 5 4 3 2 1
B. 5 3 1 4 2
C. 3 5 4 2 1
D. 3 1 4 2 5

Question 23   23.____

1. One of the most easily manipulated substances on earth, glass can be made into ceramic tiles that are composed of over 90% air.
2. NASA's space shuttles are the first spacecraft ever designed to leave and re-enter the earth's atmosphere while remaining intact.
3. These ceramic tiles are such effective insulators that when a tile emerges from the oven in which it was fired, it can be held safely in a person's hand by the edges while its interior still glows at a temperature well over 2000° F.
4. Eventually, the engineers were led to a material that is as old as our most ancient civiliza-tionsglass.
5. Because the temperature during atmospheric re-entry is so incredibly hot, it took NASA's engineers some time to find a substance capable of protecting the shuttles.

The best order is

A. 5 2 1 3 4
B. 2 5 4 1 3
C. 2 3 1 2 5
D. 5 4 3 1 2

Question 24   24.____

1. The secret to teaching any parakeet to talk is patience, and the understanding that when a bird "talks," it is simply imitating what it hears, rather than putting ideas into words.
2. You should stay just out of sight of the bird and repeat the phrase you want it to learn, for at least fifteen minutes every morning and evening.
3. It is important to leave the bird without any words of encouragement or farewell; otherwise it might combine stray remarks or phrases, such as "Good night," with the phrase you are trying to teach it.
4. For this reason, to train your bird to imitate your words you should keep it free of any dis-tractions, especially other noises, while you are giving it "lessons."
5. After your repetition, you should quietly leave the bird alone for a while, to think over what it has just heard.

The best order is

A. 1 4 2 5 3
B. 1 2 4 3 5
C. 3 2 1 5 4
D. 3 1 5 4 2

Question 25   25.____

1. As a school approaches, fishermen from neighboring communities join their fishing boats together as a fleet, and string their gill nets together to make a huge fence that is held up by cork floats.
2. At a signal from the party leaders, or *nakura,* the family members pound the sides of the boats or beat the water with long poles, creating a sudden and deafening noise.
3. The fishermen work together to drag the trap into a half-circle that may reach 300 yards in diameter, and then the families move their boats to form the other half of the circle around the school of fish.
4. The school of fish flee from the commotion into the awaiting trap, where a final wall of net is thrown over the open end of the half-circle, securing the day's haul.
5. Indonesian people from the area around the Sulu islands live on the sea, in floating villages made of lashed-together or stilted homes, and make much of their living by fishing their home waters for migrating schools of snapper, scad, and other fish.

The best order is

A. 1 5 3 4 2
B. 1 2 4 3 5
C. 5 1 2 3 4
D. 5 1 3 2 4

———

KEY (CORRECT ANSWERS)

1.	D	11.	C
2.	D	12.	A
3.	B	13.	D
4.	A	14.	C
5.	C	15.	D
6.	C	16.	C
7.	D	17.	A
8.	D	18.	D
9.	A	19.	B
10.	B	20.	A

21.	A
22.	C
23.	B
24.	A
25.	D

———

131

PHILOSOPHY, PRINCIPLES, PRACTICES AND TECHNICS
OF
SUPERVISION, ADMINISTRATION, MANAGEMENT AND ORGANIZATION

TABLE OF CONTENTS

Page

I. MEANING OF SUPERVISION 1

II. THE OLD AND THE NEW SUPERVISION 1

III. THE EIGHT (8) BASIC PRINCIPLES OF THE NEW
SUPERVISION 1
1. Principle of Responsibility 1
2. Principle of Authority 2
3. Principle of Self-Growth 2
4. Principle of Individual Worth 2
5. Principle of Creative Leadership 2
6. Principle of Success and Failure 2
7. Principle of Science 3
8. Principle of Cooperation 3

IV. WHAT IS ADMINISTRATION? 3
1. Practices commonly classed as "Supervisory" 3
2. Practices commonly classed as "Administrative" 3
3. Practices classified as both "Supervisory" and "Administrative" 4

V. RESPONSIBILITIES OF THE SUPERVISOR 4

VI. COMPETENCIES OF THE SUPERVISOR 4

VII. THE PROFESSIONAL SUPERVISOR—EMPLOYEE RELATIONSHIP 4

VIII. MINI-TEXT IN SUPERVISION, ADMINISTRATION, MANAGEMENT
AND ORGANIZATION 5
A. Brief Highlights 5
1. Levels of Management 5
2. What the Supervisor Must Learn 6
3. A Definition of Supervision 6
4. Elements of the Team Concept 6
5. Principles of Organization 6
6. The Four Important Parts of Every Job 6
7. Principles of Delegation 6
8. Principles of Effective Communications 7
9. Principles of Work Improvement 7

TABLE OF CONTENTS (CONTINUED)

10. Areas of Job Improvement 7
11. Seven Key Points in Making Improvements 7
12. Corrective Techniques for Job Improvement 7
13. A Planning Checklist 8
14. Five Characteristics of Good Directions 8
15. Types of Directions 8
16. Controls 8
17. Orienting the New Employee 8
18. Checklist for Orienting New Employees 8
19. Principles of Learning 9
20. Causes of Poor Performance 9
21. Four Major Steps in On-The-Job Instructions 9
22. Employees Want Five Things 9
23. Some Don'ts in Regard to Praise 9
24. How to Gain Your Workers' Confidence 9
25. Sources of Employee Problems 9
26. The Supervisor's Key to Discipline 10
27. Five Important Processes of Management 10
28. When the Supervisor Fails to Plan 10
29. Fourteen General Principles of Management 10
30. Change 10

B. Brief Topical Summaries 11
    I.   Who/What is the Supervisor? 11
    II.   The Sociology of Work 11
    III.   Principles and Practices of Supervision 12
    IV.   Dynamic Leadership 12
    V.   Processes for Solving Problems 12
    VI.   Training for Results 13
    VII. Health, Safety and Accident Prevention 13
    VIII. Equal Employment Opportunity 13
    IX.   Improving Communications 14
    X.   Self-Development 14
    XI.   Teaching and Training 14
        A. The Teaching Process 14
            1. Preparation 14
            2. Presentation 15
            3. Summary 15
            4. Application 15
            5. Evaluation 15
        B. Teaching Methods 15
            1. Lecture 15
            2. Discussion 15
            3. Demonstration 16
            4. Performance 16
            5. Which Method to Use 16

PHILOSOPHY, PRINCIPLES, PRACTICES, AND TECHNICS
OF
SUPERVISION, ADMINISTRATION, MANAGEMENT AND ORGANIZATION

I. MEANING OF SUPERVISION

The extension of the democratic philosophy has been accompanied by an extension in the scope of supervision. Modern leaders and supervisors no longer think of supervision in the narrow sense of being confined chiefly to visiting employees, supplying materials, or rating the staff. They regard supervision as being intimately related to all the concerned agencies of society, they speak of the supervisor's function in terms of "growth", rather than the "improvement," of employees.

This modern concept of supervision may be defined as follows:

Supervision is leadership and the development of leadership within groups which are cooperatively engaged in inspection, research, training, guidance and evaluation.

II. THE OLD AND THE NEW SUPERVISION

TRADITIONAL
1. Inspection
2. Focused on the employee
3. Visitation
4. Random and haphazard
5. Imposed and authoritarian
6. One person usually

MODERN
1. Study and analysis
2. Focused on aims, materials, methods, supervisors, employees, environment
3. Demonstrations, intervisitation, workshops, directed reading, bulletins, etc.
4. Definitely organized and planned (scientific)
5. Cooperative and democratic
6. Many persons involved (creative)

III THE EIGHT (8) BASIC PRINCIPLES OF THE NEW SUPERVISION

1. *PRINCIPLE OF RESPONSIBILITY*
   Authority to act and responsibility for acting must be joined.
   a. If you give responsibility, give authority.
   b. Define employee duties clearly.
   c. Protect employees from criticism by others.
   d. Recognize the rights as well as obligations of employees.
   e. Achieve the aims of a democratic society insofar as it is possible within the area of your work.
   f. Establish a situation favorable to training and learning.
   g. Accept ultimate responsibility for everything done in your section, unit, office, division, department.
   h. Good administration and good supervision are inseparable.

2. PRINCIPLE OF AUTHORITY

The success of the supervisor is measured by the extent to which the power of authority is not used.

a. Exercise simplicity and informality in supervision.
b. Use the simplest machinery of supervision.
c. If it is good for the organization as a whole, it is probably justified.
d. Seldom be arbitrary or authoritative.
e. Do not base your work on the power of position or of personality.
f. Permit and encourage the free expression of opinions.

3. PRINCIPLE OF SELF-GROWTH

The success of the supervisor is measured by the extent to which, and the speed with which, he is no longer needed.

a. Base criticism on principles, not on specifics.
b. Point out higher activities to employees.
c. Train for self-thinking by employees, to meet new situations.
d. Stimulate initiative, self-reliance and individual responsibility.
e. Concentrate on stimulating the growth of employees rather than on removing defects.

4. PRINCIPLE OF INDIVIDUAL WORTH

Respect for the individual is a paramount consideration in supervision.

a. Be human and sympathetic in dealing with employees.
b. Don't nag about things to be done.
c. Recognize the individual differences among employees and seek opportunities to permit best expression of each personality.

5. PRINCIPLE OF CREATIVE LEADERSHIP

The best supervision is that which is not apparent to the employee.

a. Stimulate, don't drive employees to creative action.
b. Emphasize doing good things.
c. Encourage employees to do what they do best.
d. Do not be too greatly concerned with details of subject or method.
e. Do not be concerned exclusively with immediate problems and activities.
f. Reveal higher activities and make them both desired and maximally possible.
g. Determine procedures in the light of each situation but see that these are derived from a sound basic philosophy.
h. Aid, inspire and lead so as to liberate the creative spirit latent in all good employees.

6. PRINCIPLE OF SUCCESS AND FAILURE

There are no unsuccessful employees, only unsuccessful supervisors who have failed to give proper leadership.

a. Adapt suggestions to the capacities, attitudes, and prejudices of employees.
b. Be gradual, be progressive, be persistent.
c. Help the employee find the general principle; have the employee apply his own problem to the general principle.
d. Give adequate appreciation for good work and honest effort.
e. Anticipate employee difficulties and help to prevent them.
f. Encourage employees to do the desirable things they will do anyway.
g. Judge your supervision by the results it secures.

7. PRINCIPLE OF SCIENCE

Successful supervision is scientific, objective, and experimental. It is based on facts, not on prejudices.

  a. Be cumulative in results.
  b. Never divorce your suggestions from the goals of training.
  c. Don't be impatient of results.
  d. Keep all matters on a professional, not a personal level.
  e. Do not be concerned exclusively with immediate problems and activities.
  f. Use objective means of determining achievement and rating where possible.

8. PRINCIPLE OF COOPERATION

Supervision is a cooperative enterprise between supervisor and employee.

  a. Begin with conditions as they are.
  b. Ask opinions of all involved when formulating policies.
  c. Organization is as good as its weakest link.
  d. Let employees help to determine policies and department programs.
  e. Be approachable and accessible - physically and mentally.
  f. Develop pleasant social relationships.

IV. WHAT IS ADMINISTRATION?

Administration is concerned with providing the environment, the material facilities, and the operational procedures that will promote the maximum growth and development of supervisors and employees. (Organization is an aspect, and a concomitant, of administration.)

There is no sharp line of demarcation between supervision and administration; these functions are intimately interrelated and, often, overlapping. They are complementary activities.

1. PRACTICES COMMONLY CLASSED AS "SUPERVISORY"

  a. Conducting employees conferences
  b. Visiting sections, units, offices, divisions, departments
  c. Arranging for demonstrations
  d. Examining plans
  e. Suggesting professional reading
  f. Interpreting bulletins
  g. Recommending in-service training courses
  h. Encouraging experimentation
  i. Appraising employee morale
  j. Providing for intervisitation

2. PRACTICES COMMONLY CLASSIFIED AS "ADMINISTRATIVE"

  a. Management of the office
  b. Arrangement of schedules for extra duties
  c. Assignment of rooms or areas
  d. Distribution of supplies
  e. Keeping records and reports
  f. Care of audio-visual materials
  g. Keeping inventory records
  h. Checking record cards and books
  i. Programming special activities
  j. Checking on the attendance and punctuality of employees

3. *PRACTICES COMMONLY CLASSIFIED AS BOTH "SUPERVISORY" AND "ADMINISTRATIVE"*
    a. Program construction
    b. Testing or evaluating outcomes
    c. Personnel accounting
    d. Ordering instructional materials

V. RESPONSIBILITIES OF THE SUPERVISOR

A person employed in a supervisory capacity must constantly be able to improve his own efficiency and ability. He represents the employer to the employees and only continuous self-examination can make him a capable supervisor.

Leadership and training are the supervisor's responsibility. An efficient working unit is one in which the employees work with the supervisor. It is his job to bring out the best in his employees. He must always be relaxed, courteous and calm in his association with his employees. Their feelings are important, and a harsh attitude does not develop the most efficient employees.

VI. COMPETENCIES OF THE SUPERVISOR

1. Complete knowledge of the duties and responsibilities of his position.
2. To be able to organize a job, plan ahead and carry through.
3. To have self-confidence and initiative.
4. To be able to handle the unexpected situation and make quick decisions.
5. To be able to properly train subordinates in the positions they are best suited for.
6. To be able to keep good human relations among his subordinates.
7. To be able to keep good human relations between his subordinates and himself and to earn their respect and trust.

VII. THE PROFESSIONAL SUPERVISOR-EMPLOYEE RELATIONSHIP

There are two kinds of efficiency: one kind is only apparent and is produced in organizations through the exercise of mere discipline; this is but a simulation of the second, or true, efficiency which springs from spontaneous cooperation. If you are a manager, no matter how great or small your responsibility, it is your job, in the final analysis, to create and develop this involuntary cooperation among the people whom you supervise. For, no matter how powerful a combination of money, machines, and materials a company may have, this is a dead and sterile thing without a team of willing, thinking and articulate people to guide it.

The following 21 points are presented as indicative of the exemplary basic relationship that should exist between supervisor and employee:

1. Each person wants to be liked and respected by his fellow employee and wants to be treated with consideration and respect by his superior.
2. The most competent employee will make an error. However, in a unit where good relations exist between the supervisor and his employees, tenseness and fear do not exist. Thus, errors are not hidden or covered up and the efficiency of a unit is not impaired.
3. Subordinates resent rules, regulations, or orders that are unreasonable or unexplained.
4. Subordinates are quick to resent unfairness, harshness, injustices and favoritism.
5. An employee will accept responsibility if he knows that he will be complimented for a job well done, and not too harshly chastised for failure; that his supervisor will check the cause of the failure, and, if it was the supervisor's fault, he will assume the blame therefore. If it was the employee's fault, his supervisor will explain the correct method or means of handling the responsibility.

6. An employee wants to receive credit for a suggestion he has made, that is used. If a suggestion cannot be used, the employee is entitled to an explanation. The supervisor should not say "no" and close the subject.
7. Fear and worry slow up a worker's ability. Poor working environment can impair his physical and mental health. A good supervisor avoids forceful methods, threats and arguments to get a job done.
8. A forceful supervisor is able to train his employees individually and as a team, and is able to motivate them in the proper channels.
9. A mature supervisor is able to properly evaluate his subordinates and to keep them happy and satisfied.
10. A sensitive supervisor will never patronize his subordinates.
11. A worthy supervisor will respect his employees' confidences.
12. Definite and clear-cut responsibilities should be assigned to each executive.
13. Responsibility should always be coupled with corresponding authority.
14. No change should be made in the scope or responsibilities of a position without a definite understanding to that effect on the part of all persons concerned.
15. No executive or employee, occupying a single position in the organization, should be subject to definite orders from more than one source.
16. Orders should never be given to subordinates over the head of a responsible executive. Rather than do this, the officer in question should be supplanted.
17. Criticisms of subordinates should, whoever possible, be made privately, and in no case should a subordinate be criticized in the presence of executives or employees of equal or lower rank.
18. No dispute or difference between executives or employees as to authority or responsibilities should be considered too trivial for prompt and careful adjudication.
19. Promotions, wage changes, and disciplinary action should always be approved by the executive immediately superior to the one directly responsible.
20. No executive or employee should ever be required, or expected, to be at the same time an assistant to, and critic of, another.
21. Any executive whose work is subject to regular inspection should, whever practicable, be given the assistance and facilities necessary to enable him to maintain an independent check of the quality of his work.

VIII. MINI-TEXT IN SUPERVISION, ADMINISTRATION, MANAGEMENT, AND ORGANIZATION

A. BRIEF HIGHLIGHTS

Listed concisely and sequentially are major headings and important data in the field for quick recall and review.

1. *LEVELS OF MANAGEMENT*
Any organization of some size has several levels of management. In terms of a ladder the levels are:

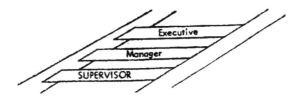

The first level is very important because it is the beginning point of management leadership.

2. WHAT THE SUPERVISOR MUST LEARN

A supervisor must learn to:

(1) Deal with people and their differences
(2) Get the job done through people
(3) Recognize the problems when they exist
(4) Overcome obstacles to good performance
(5) Evaluate the performance of people
(6) Check his own performance in terms of accomplishment

3. A DEFINITION OF SUPERVISOR

The term supervisor means any individual having authority, in the interests of the employer, to hire, transfer, suspend, lay-off, recall, promote, discharge, assign, reward, or discipline other employees or responsibility to direct them, or to adjust their grievances, or effectively to recommend such action, if, in connection with the foregoing, exercise of such authority is not of a merely routine or clerical nature but requires the use of independent judgment.

4. ELEMENTS OF THE TEAM CONCEPT

What is involved in teamwork? The component parts are:

(1) Members   (3) Goals   (5) Cooperation
(2) A leader   (4) Plans   (6) Spirit

5. PRINCIPLES OF ORGANIZATION

(1) A team member must know what his job is.
(2) Be sure that the nature and scope of a job are understood.
(3) Authority and responsibility should be carefully spelled out.
(4) A supervisor should be permitted to make the maximum number of decisions affecting his employees.
(5) Employees should report to only one supervisor.
(6) A supervisor should direct only as many employees as he can handle effectively.
(7) An organization plan should be flexible.
(8) Inspection and performance of work should be separate.
(9) Organizational problems should receive immediate attention.
(10) Assign work in line with ability and experience.

6. THE FOUR IMPORTANT PARTS OF EVERY JOB

(1) Inherent in every job is the *accountability* for results.
(2) A second set of factors in every job is *responsibilities.*
(3) Along with duties and responsibilities one must have the *authority* to act within certain limits without obtaining permission to proceed.
(4) No job exists in a vacuum. The supervisor is surrounded by key *relationships.*

7. PRINCIPLES OF DELEGATION

Where work is delegated for the first time, the supervisor should think in terms of these questions:

(1) Who is best qualified to do this?
(2) Can an employee improve his abilities by doing this?
(3) How long should an employee spend on this?
(4) Are there any special problems for which he will need guidance?
(5) How broad a delegation can I make?

8. PRINCIPLES OF EFFECTIVE COMMUNICATIONS
    (1) Determine the media
    (2) To whom directed?
    (3) Identification and source authority
    (4) Is communication understood?

9. PRINCIPLES OF WORK IMPROVEMENT
    (1) Most people usually do only the work which is assigned to them
    (2) Workers are likely to fit assigned work into the time available to perform it
    (3) A good workload usually stimulates output
    (4) People usually do their best work when they know that results will be reviewed or inspected
    (5) Employees usually feel that someone else is responsible for conditions of work, workplace layout, job methods, type of tools/equipment, and other such factors
    (6) Employees are usually defensive about their job security
    (7) Employees have natural resistance to change
    (8) Employees can support or destroy a supervisor
    (9) A supervisor usually earns the respect of his people through his personal example of diligence and efficiency

10. AREAS OF JOB IMPROVEMENT
The areas of job improvement are quite numerous, but the most common ones which a supervisor can identify and utilize are:

    (1) Departmental layout   (5) Work methods
    (2) Flow of work   (6) Materials handling
    (3) Workplace layout   (7) Utilization
    (4) Utilization of manpower   (8) Motion economy

11. SEVEN KEY POINTS IN MAKING IMPROVEMENTS
    (1) Select the job to be improved
    (2) Study how it is being done now
    (3) Question the present method
    (4) Determine actions to be taken
    (5) Chart proposed method
    (6) Get approval and apply
    (7) Solicit worker participation

12. CORRECTIVE TECHNIQUES OF JOB IMPROVEMENT

Specific Problems	General Improvement	Corrective Techniques
(1) Size of workload	(1) Departmental layout	(1) Study with scale model
(2) Inability to meet schedules	(2) Flow of work	(2) Flow chart study
(3) Strain and fatigue	(3) Work plan layout	(3) Motion analysis
(4) Improper use of men and skills	(4) Utilization of manpower	(4) Comparison of units produced to standard allowance
(5) Waste, poor quality, unsafe conditions	(5) Work methods	(5) Methods analysis
(6) Bottleneck conditions that hinder output	(6) Materials handling	(6) Flow chart & equipment study
(7) Poor utilization of equipment and machine	(7) Utilization of equipment	(7) Down time vs. running time
(8) Efficiency and productivity of labor	(8) Motion economy	(8) Motion analysis

13. A *PLANNING CHECKLIST*

(1) Objectives	(6) Resources	(11) Safety
(2) Controls	(7) Manpower	(12) Money
(3) Delegations	(8) Equipment	(13) Work
(4) Communications	(9) Supplies and materials	(14) Timing of improvements
(5) Resources	(10) Utilization of time	

14. *FIVE CHARACTERISTICS OF GOOD DIRECTIONS*

In order to get results, directions must be:

(1) Possible of accomplishment	(3) Related to mission	(5) Unmistakably clear
(2) Agreeable with worker interests	(4) Planned and complete	

15. *TYPES OF DIRECTIONS*

(1) Demands or direct orders	(3) Suggestion or implication
(2) Requests	(4) Volunteering

16. *CONTROLS*

A typical listing of the overall areas in which the supervisor should establish controls might be:

(1) Manpower	(3) Quality of work	(5) Time	(7) Money
(2) Materials	(4) Quantity of work	(6) Space	(8) Methods

17. *ORIENTING THE NEW EMPLOYEE*

(1) Prepare for him	(3) Orientation for the job
(2) Welcome the new employee	(4) Follow-up

18. *CHECKLIST FOR ORIENTING NEW EMPLOYEES*

	Yes	No
(1) Do your appreciate the feelings of new employees when they first report for work?	____	____
(2) Are you aware of the fact that the new employee must make a big adjustment to his job?	____	____
(3) Have you given him good reasons for liking the job and the organization?	____	____
(4) Have you prepared for his first day on the job?		
(5) Did you welcome him cordially and make him feel needed?		
(6) Did you establish rapport with him so that he feels free to talk and discuss matters with you?	____	____
(7) Did you explain his job to him and his relationship to you?	____	____
(8) Does he know that his work will be evaluated periodically on a basis that is fair and objective?	____	____
(9) Did you introduce him to his fellow workers in such a way that they are likely to accept him?	____	____
(10) Does he know what employee benefits he will receive?		
(11) Does he understand the importance of being on the job and what to do if he must leave his duty station?	____	____
(12) Has he been impressed with the importance of accident prevention and safe practice?	____	____
(13) Does he generally know his way around the department?	____	____
(14) Is he under the guidance of a sponsor who will teach the right ways of doing things?	____	____
(15) Do you plan to follow-up so that he will continue to adjust successfully to his job?	____	____

19. PRINCIPLES OF LEARNING
(1) Motivation   (2) Demonstration or explanation   (3) Practice

20. CAUSES OF POOR PERFORMANCE
(1) Improper training for job
(2) Wrong tools
(3) Inadequate directions
(4) Lack of supervisory follow-up
(5) Poor communications
(6) Lack of standards of performance
(7) Wrong work habits
(8) Low morale
(9) Other

21. FOUR MAJOR STEPS IN ON-THE-JOB INSTRUCTION
(1) Prepare the worker
(2) Present the operation
(3) Tryout performance
(4) Follow-up

22. EMPLOYEES WANT FIVE THINGS
(1) Security (2) Opportunity (3) Recognition (4) Inclusion (5) Expression

23. SOME DON'TS IN REGARD TO PRAISE
(1) Don't praise a person for something he hasn't done
(2) Don't praise a person unless you can be sincere
(3) Don't be sparing in praise just because your superior withholds it from you
(4) Don't let too much time elapse between good performance and recognition of it

24. HOW TO GAIN YOUR WORKERS' CONFIDENCE
Methods of developing confidence include such things as:
(1) Knowing the interests, habits, hobbies of employees
(2) Admitting your own inadequacies
(3) Sharing and telling of confidence in others
(4) Supporting people when they are in trouble
(5) Delegating matters that can be well handled
(6) Being frank and straightforward about problems and working conditions
(7) Encouraging others to bring their problems to you
(8) Taking action on problems which impede worker progress

25. SOURCES OF EMPLOYEE PROBLEMS
On-the-job causes might be such things as:
(1) A feeling that favoritism is exercised in assignments
(2) Assignment of overtime
(3) An undue amount of supervision
(4) Changing methods or systems
(5) Stealing of ideas or trade secrets
(6) Lack of interest in job
(7) Threat of reduction in force
(8) Ignorance or lack of communications
(9) Poor equipment
(10) Lack of knowing how supervisor feels toward employee
(11) Shift assignments

Off-the-job problems might have to do with:
(1) Health   (2) Finances   (3) Housing   (4) Family

26. *THE SUPERVISOR'S KEY TO DISCIPLINE*

There are several key points about discipline which the supervisor should keep in mind:

(1) Job discipline is one of the disciplines of life and is directed by the supervisor.

(2) It is more important to correct an employee fault than to fix blame for it.

(3) Employee performance is affected by problems both on the job and off.

(4) Sudden or abrupt changes in behavior can be indications of important employee problems.

(5) Problems should be dealt with as soon as possible after they are identified.

(6) The attitude of the supervisor may have more to do with solving problems than the techniques of problem solving.

(7) Correction of employee behavior should be resorted to only after the supervisor is sure that training or counseling will not be helpful.

(8) Be sure to document your disciplinary actions.

(9) Make sure that you are disciplining on the basis of facts rather than personal feelings.

(10) Take each disciplinary step in order, being careful not to make snap judgments, or decisions based on impatience.

27. *FIVE IMPORTANT PROCESSES OF MANAGEMENT*

(1) Planning   (2) Organizing   (3) Scheduling
(4) Controlling (5) Motivating

28. *WHEN THE SUPERVISOR FAILS TO PLAN*

(1) Supervisor creates impression of not knowing his job

(2) May lead to excessive overtime

(3) Job runs itself -- supervisor lacks control

(4) Deadlines and appointments missed

(5) Parts of the work go undone

(6) Work interrupted by emergencies

(7) Sets a bad example

(8) Uneven workload creates peaks and valleys

(9) Too much time on minor details at expense of more important tasks

29. *FOURTEEN GENERAL PRINCIPLES OF MANAGEMENT*

(1) Division of work

(2) Authority and responsibility

(3) Discipline

(4) Unity of command

(5) Unity of direction

(6) Subordination of individual interest to general interest

(7) Remuneration of personnel

(8) Centralization

(9) Scalar chain

(10) Order

(11) Equity

(12) Stability of tenure of personnel

(13) Initiative

(14) Esprit de corps

30. *CHANGE*

Bringing about change is perhaps attempted more often, and yet less well understood, than anything else the supervisor does. How do people generally react to change? (People tend to resist change that is imposed upon them by other individuals or circumstances.

Change is characteristic of every situation. It is a part of every real endeavor where the efforts of people are concerned.

144

A. Why do people resist change?
   People may resist change because of:
   (1) Fear of the unknown
   (2) Implied criticism
   (3) Unpleasant experiences in the past
   (4) Fear of loss of status
   (5) Threat to the ego
   (6) Fear of loss of economic stability

B. How can we best overcome the resistance to change?
   In initiating change, take these steps:
   (1) Get ready to sell
   (2) Identify sources of help
   (3) Anticipate objections
   (4) Sell benefits
   (5) Listen in depth
   (6) Follow up

B. BRIEF TOPICAL SUMMARIES

I. WHO/WHAT IS THE SUPERVISOR?

1. The supervisor is often called the "highest level employee and the lowest level manager."
2. A supervisor is a member of both management and the work group. He acts as a bridge between the two.
3. Most problems in supervision are in the area of human relations, or people problems.
4. Employees expect: Respect, opportunity to learn and to advance, and a sense of belonging, and so forth.
5. Supervisors are responsible for directing people and organizing work. Planning is of paramount importance.
6. A position description is a set of duties and responsibilities inherent to a given position.
7. It is important to keep the position description up-to-date and to provide each employee with his own copy.

II. THE SOCIOLOGY OF WORK

1. People are alike in many ways; however, each individual is unique.
2. The supervisor is challenged in getting to know employee differences. Acquiring skills in evaluating individuals is an asset.
3. Maintaining meaningful working relationships in the organization is of great importance.
4. The supervisor has an obligation to help individuals to develop to their fullest potential.
5. Job rotation on a planned basis helps to build versatility and to maintain interest and enthusiasm in work groups.
6. Cross training (job rotation) provides backup skills.
7. The supervisor can help reduce tension by maintaining a sense of humor, providing guidance to employees, and by making reasonable and timely decisions. Employees respond favorably to working under reasonably predictable circumstances.
8. Change is characteristic of all managerial behavior. The supervisor must adjust to changes in procedures, new methods, technological changes, and to a number of new and sometimes challenging situations.
9. To overcome the natural tendency for people to resist change, the supervisor should become more skillful in initiating change.

III. PRINCIPLES AND PRACTICES OF SUPERVISION

1. Employees should be required to answer to only one superior.
2. A supervisor can effectively direct only a limited number of employees, depending upon the complexity, variety, and proximity of the jobs involved.
3. The organizational chart presents the organization in graphic form. It reflects lines of authority and responsibility as well as interrelationships of units within the organization.
4. Distribution of work can be improved through an analysis using the "Work Distribution Chart."
5. The "Work Distribution Chart" reflects the division of work within a unit in understandable form.
6. When related tasks are given to an employee, he has a better chance of increasing his skills through training.
7. The individual who is given the responsibility for tasks must also be given the appropriate authority to insure adequate results.
8. The supervisor should delegate repetitive, routine work. Preparation of recurring reports, maintaining leave and attendance records are some examples.
9. Good discipline is essential to good task performance. Discipline is reflected in the actions of employees on the job in the absence of supervision.
10. Disciplinary action may have to be taken when the positive aspects of discipline have failed. Reprimand, warning, and suspension are examples of disciplinary action.
11. If a situation calls for a reprimand, be sure it is deserved and remember it is to be done in private.

IV. DYNAMIC LEADERSHIP

1. A style is a personal method or manner of exerting influence.
2. Authoritarian leaders often see themselves as the source of power and authority.
3. The democratic leader often perceives the group as the source of authority and power.
4. Supervisors tend to do better when using the pattern of leadership that is most natural for them.
5. Social scientists suggest that the effective supervisor use the leadership style that best fits the problem or circumstances involved.
6. All four styles -- telling, selling, consulting, joining -- have their place. Using one does not preclude using the other at another time.
7. The theory X point of view assumes that the average person dislikes work, will avoid it whenever possible, and must be coerced to achieve organizational objectives.
8. The theory Y point of view assumes that the average person considers work to be as natural as play, and, when the individual is committed, he requires little supervision or direction to accomplish desired objectives.
9. The leader's basic assumptions concerning human behavior and human nature affect his actions, decisions, and other managerial practices.
10. Dissatisfaction among employees is often present, but difficult to isolate. The supervisor should seek to weaken dissatisfaction by keeping promises, being sincere and considerate, keeping employees informed, and so forth.
11. Constructive suggestions should be encouraged during the natural progress of the work.

V. PROCESSES FOR SOLVING PROBLEMS

1. People find their daily tasks more meaningful and satisfying when they can improve them.
2. The causes of problems, or the key factors, are often hidden in the background. Ability to solve problems often involves the ability to isolate them from their backgrounds. There is some substance to the cliché that some persons "can't see the forest for the trees."
3. New procedures are often developed from old ones. Problems should be broken down into manageable parts. New ideas can be adapted from old ones.

4. People think differently in problem-solving situations. Using a logical, patterned approach is often useful. One approach found to be useful includes these steps:

    (a) Define the problem   (d) Weigh and decide
    (b) Establish objectives   (e) Take action
    (c) Get the facts   (f) Evaluate action

VI. TRAINING FOR RESULTS

1. Participants respond best when they feel training is important to them.
2. The supervisor has responsibility for the training and development of those who report to him.
3. When training is delegated to others, great care must be exercised to insure the trainer has knowledge, aptitude, and interest for his work as a trainer.
4. Training (learning) of some type goes on continually. The most successful supervisor makes certain the learning contributes in a productive manner to operational goals.
5. New employees are particularly susceptible to training. Older employees facing new job situations require specific training, as well as having need for development and growth opportunities.
6. Training needs require continuous monitoring.
7. The training officer of an agency is a professional with a responsibility to assist supervisors in solving training problems.
8. Many of the self-development steps important to the supervisor's own growth are equally important to the development of peers and subordinates. Knowledge of these is important when the supervisor consults with others on development and growth opportunities.

VII. HEALTH, SAFETY, AND ACCIDENT PREVENTION

1. Management-minded supervisors take appropriate measures to assist employees in maintaining health and in assuring safe practices in the work environment.
2. Effective safety training and practices help to avoid injury and accidents.
3. Safety should be a management goal. All infractions of safety which are observed should be corrected without exception.
4. Employees' safety attitude, training and instruction, provision of safe tools and equipment, supervision, and leadership are considered highly important factors which contribute to safety and which can be influenced directly by supervisors.
5. When accidents do occur they should be investigated promptly for very important reasons, including the fact that information which is gained can be used to prevent accidents in the future.

VIII. EQUAL EMPLOYMENT OPPORTUNITY

1. The supervisor should endeavor to treat all employees fairly, without regard to religion, race, sex, or national origin.
2. Groups tend to reflect the attitude of the leader. Prejudice can be detected even in very subtle form. Supervisors must strive to create a feeling of mutual respect and confidence in every employee.
3. Complete utilization of all human resources is a national goal. Equitable consideration should be accorded women in the work force, minority-group members, the physically and mentally handicapped, and the older employee. The important question is: "Who can do the job?"
4. Training opportunities, recognition for performance, overtime assignments, promotional opportunities, and all other personnel actions are to be handled on an equitable basis.

IX. IMPROVING COMMUNICATIONS

1. Communications is achieving understanding between the sender and the receiver of a message. It also means sharing information -- the creation of understanding.
2. Communication is basic to all human activity. Words are means of conveying meanings; however, real meanings are in people.
3. There are very practical differences in the effectiveness of one-way, impersonal, and two-way communications. Words spoken face-to-face are better understood. Telephone conversations are effective, but lack the rapport of person-to-person exchanges. The whole person communicates.
4. Cooperation and communication in an organization go hand in hand. When there is a mutual respect between people, spelling out rules and procedures for communicating is unnecessary.
5. There are several barriers to effective communications. These include failure to listen with respect and understanding, lack of skill in feedback, and misinterpreting the meanings of words used by the speaker. It is also common practice to listen to what we want to hear, and tune out things we do not want to hear.
6. Communication is management's chief problem. The supervisor should accept the challenge to communicate more effectively and to improve interagency and intra-agency communications.
7. The supervisor may often plan for and conduct meetings. The planning phase is critical and may determine the success or the failure of a meeting.
8. Speaking before groups usually requires extra effort. Stage fright may never disappear completely, but it can be controlled.

X. SELF-DEVELOPMENT

1. Every employee is responsible for his own self-development.
2. Toastmaster and toastmistress clubs offer opportunities to improve skills in oral communications.
3. Planning for one's own self-development is of vital importance. Supervisors know their own strengths and limitations better than anyone else.
4. Many opportunities are open to aid the supervisor in his developmental efforts, including job assignments; training opportunities, both governmental and non-governmental -- to include universities and professional conferences and seminars.
5. Programmed instruction offers a means of studying at one's own rate.
6. Where difficulties may arise from a supervisor's being away from his work for training, he may participate in televised home study or correspondence courses to meet his self-develop- ment needs.

XI. TEACHING AND TRAINING

A. The Teaching Process

Teaching is encouraging and guiding the learning activities of students toward established goals. In most cases this process consists in five steps: preparation, presentation, summarization, evaluation, and application.

1. Preparation
Preparation is twofold in nature; that of the supervisor and the employee.
Preparation by the supervisor is absolutely essential to success. He must know what, when, where, how, and whom he will teach. Some of the factors that should be considered are:

   (1) The objectives   (5) Employee interest
   (2) The materials needed   (6) Training aids
   (3) The methods to be used   (7) Evaluation
   (4) Employee participation   (8) Summarization

Employee preparation consists in preparing the employee to receive the material. Probably the most important single factor in the preparation of the employee is arousing and maintaining his interest. He must know the objectives of the training, why he is there, how the material can be used, and its importance to him.

2. Presentation

In presentation, have a carefully designed plan and follow it.
The plan should be accurate and complete, yet flexible enough to meet situations as they arise. The method of presentation will be determined by the particular situation and objectives.

3. Summary

A summary should be made at the end of every training unit and program. In addition, there may be internal summaries depending on the nature of the material being taught. The important thing is that the trainee must always be able to understand how each part of the new material relates to the whole.

4. Application

The supervisor must arrange work so the employee will be given a chance to apply new knowledge or skills while the material is still clear in his mind and interest is high. The trainee does not really know whether he has learned the material until he has been given a chance to apply it. If the material is not applied, it loses most of its value.

5. Evaluation

The purpose of all training is to promote learning. To determine whether the training has been a success or failure, the supervisor must evaluate this learning.

In the broadest sense evaluation includes all the devices, methods, skills, and techniques used by the supervisor to keep him self and the employees informed as to their progress toward the objectives they are pursuing. The extent to which the employee has mastered the knowledge, skills, and abilities, or changed his attitudes, as determined by the program objectives, is the extent to which instruction has succeeded or failed.

Evaluation should not be confined to the end of the lesson, day, or program but should be used continuously. We shall note later the way this relates to the rest of the teaching process.

B. Teaching Methods

A teaching method is a pattern of identifiable student and instructor activity used in presenting training material.

All supervisors are faced with the problem of deciding which method should be used at a given time.

As with all methods, there are certain advantages and disadvantages to each method.

1. Lecture

The lecture is direct oral presentation of material by the supervisor. The present trend is to place less emphasis on the trainer's activity and more on that of the trainee.

2. Discussion

Teaching by discussion or conference involves using questions and other techniques to arouse interest and focus attention upon certain areas, and by doing so creating a learning situation. This can be one of the most valuable methods because it gives the employees 'an opportunity to express their ideas and pool their knowledge.

3. Demonstration

The demonstration is used to teach how something works or how to do something. It can be used to show a principle or what the results of a series of actions will be. A well-staged demonstration is particularly effective because it shows proper methods of performance in a realistic manner.

4. Performance

Performance is one of the most fundamental of all learning techniques or teaching methods. The trainee may be able to tell how a specific operation should be performed but he cannot be sure he knows how to perform the operation until he has done so.

5. Which Method to Use

Moreover, there are other methods and techniques of teaching. It is difficult to use any method without other methods entering into it. In any learning situation a combination of methods is usually more effective than anyone method alone.

Finally, evaluation must be integrated into the other aspects of the teaching-learning process.

It must be used in the motivation of the trainees; it must be used to assist in developing understanding during the training; and it must be related to employee application of the results of training.

This is distinctly the role of the supervisor.